Whirligigs
DESIGN AND CONSTRUCTION

Whirligigs

DESIGN AND CONSTRUCTION

SECOND EDITION

ANDERS S. LUNDE

Chilton Book Company Radnor, Pennsylvania

Copyright © 1982, 1986 by Anders S. Lunde
Second Edition
All Rights Reserved
Published in Radnor, Pennsylvania 19089, by Chilton Book Company

No part of this book may be reproduced, transmitted or stored
in any form or by any means, electronic or mechanical,
without prior written permission from the publisher

Photographs by John Rosenthal

Manufactured in the United States of America

Library of Congress Cataloging in Publication Data
Lunde, Anders S.
    Whirligigs: design and construction
    Second Edition
    Rev. ed. of Whirligigs. 1984.
    Includes index.
    1. Wooden toy making.   2. Whirligigs.   I. Lunde,
Anders S. More Whirligigs.   II. Title.
TT174.5.W6L86   1986   745.592   86-47607
ISBN 0-8019-7707-X (pbk.)

13 14 15 16 17   7 6 5 4 3 2 1

With special appreciation to Tony Lunde, whose help made this work possible, and to my grandchildren Beth, Catherine, Robbie, Jennifer, Andy, Elizabeth, and Danny

Contents

Chapter 1   Introduction to the Whirligig   1
The Original Whirligig   2
Design   3
Construction   3
    Materials   3
    Basic Tools   3
    Wood   3
    Mounting Stand   3
    Fan   4
    Labeling Parts   4
    Drafting and Copying   4
    Putting it All Together   4

Chapter 2   Types of Whirligigs   6
Winged Whirligigs   6
Arm-Waving Whirligigs   7
Weathervane Whirligigs and Other Special Types   8
Mechanical Whirligigs   9

Chapter 3   Basic Whirligig Parts   12
Body   12
Wing Base   12
Pivot   12

Propeller 13
   Basic Style 14
   Modified Propellers 14
   Multibladed Designs 15
   Metal Propellers 16
   Mechanical Styles 17
   New Designs 18
Driveshafts for Mechanical Whirligigs 20

Chapter 4   Construction of Winged Whirligigs 21
Basic Steps 21
   Design 21
   Body 21
   Wing Base 22
   Wings 22
   Assembly 23
Standard Bird Models 23
   The Cardinal 23
Split-Wing Models 25
   The Flying Puffin 26
   Other Types 26
Modified-Wing Models 27
   Modern Times 27

Chapter 5   Construction of Arm-Waving Whirligigs 41
Basic Steps 42
   Design 42
   Patterns 42
   Hub and Pivot Point 42
   Cutting and Carving 43
   Arms and Attachments 43
   Final Assembly 43
Standard Models 43
   Uncle Sam 44
   Signaling Sailor 44
   Gentleman Jim 45
   Flower Lady 46
Rudder Assembly Models 46
   Soldier, Colonial Dame, Santa and Doggie Models 46
Modified Propeller Models 49
   Man Rowing Boat 50
   Indian in Canoe 52

Chapter 6   Construction of Weathervane Whirligigs 64
Basic Steps 64
   Design 64

Patterns and Cuts   65
Balance and Pivot   65
Weathervane Models   65
Willy the Whale   67
The Flying Witch   67
The Ships   67
Georgine and Her Flying Machine   67
Halley's Comet   69

Chapter 7   Construction of Mechanical Whirligigs   77
Basic Steps   77
Individual Models   78
The Churning Woman   78
Signaling Trainman   79
Forever Grinding   80

Chapter 8   Developing Original Designs   92
Final Notes on Construction   92
Repairing Whirligigs   93
Developing New Designs   93

Index   94

Whirligigs

DESIGN AND CONSTRUCTION

1

Introduction to the Whirligig

Welcome to the wonderful world of whirligigs!

A whirligig is a device, moved by the wind, which whirls and turns around on its pivot. Most whirligigs have been small, toylike objects, often called "wind-toys." Some are quite large, from full-sized seagulls to huge contraptions which generate electricity. Many are simple in design, with a person waving arms; others have been exceedingly complicated, with several persons or animals activated at the same time on several levels of operation. Whatever its size or shape, the whirligig has two universal characteristics: it has been created for the fun of it, and it gives pleasure to those who see it.

The origin of whirligigs is a mystery. Some pinwheel types appear to have been popular in Europe in the 16th century, and it is possible that they came to Europe with the windmill, which was introduced from the East about the 12th century (Fig. 1.1).

Craftsmen in America were making simple whirligigs in the 18th and early 19th centuries, and later developed more complex designs. Models from these early periods are quite rare, because for the most part they were designed and constructed by individuals whose designs died with them. At various times, whirligigs were mass produced and distributed throughout the country; because they were made of wood and exposed to the elements, they dete-

FIG. 1.1

1

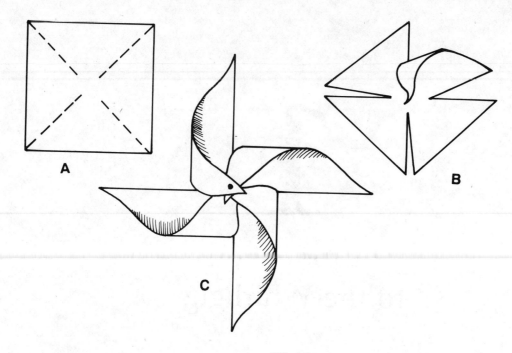

FIG. 1.2

riorated with time. This has been the case even with 20th-century models. Whirligig construction was popular during the Great Depression; in the 1930s, people with time on their hands created simple whirligigs to sell by the side of the road. Today, in the Appalachian Mountains, the tradition is being carried on as a pastime, and many craftspeople are making mechanical whirligigs as a creative hobby.

There is no limit to the designs that can be made. Everyone can create new designs or adapt old ones and is limited only by imagination. The designs in this book are original in the sense that they have been drawn, constructed, and tested by the author. Some are old American motifs: the Indian in Canoe, the Soldier waving his sword. The Woman Churning is an adaptation from a traditional North Carolina model. My grandchildren are responsible for the dragon and the dog. The whirligig maker can get many ideas from visits to folk art museums and from books containing illustrations of antique whirligigs. But often the best idea is that which comes almost unbidden to the mind, the original creative inspiration which can be translated into a work-

2

ing whirligig. Whirligigs created from these fresh ideas are truly part of a great American tradition.

THE ORIGINAL WHIRLIGIG

Everyone interested in making whirligigs should take a few moments to construct what some believe to be the first wind toy ever. This will remind the whirligig artist of some fundamentals: (1) whirligigs are for fun, (2) whirligigs are inexpensive to make, (3) whirligigs operate freely in the wind, and (4) whirligig propellers of excellent design are easy to make.

The simple spinner which was possibly the first whirligig ever is none other than the simple pinwheel. Who made the first one? A grandfather in ancient China? A mother in Persia? We will never know. All we do know is that pinwheels appeared in Europe about 500 years ago. In case you've forgotten how to make one of these ancient devices, directions are given here. Prepare a square piece of paper (5" or 6" square). With scissors, cut in from the corners to about 1" from the center. Then fold over four corners in sequence, and pin or tack the ends through the center to a stick or round piece of wood (Fig. 1.2).

Swing it through an arc or hold it to face the wind, and watch it turn. This will remind you of how old whirligigs are and of how fascinating they have been to both young and old, generation after generation.

DESIGN

The planning, designing, and drawing to scale of a whirligig is the first step in creating an original model. A full-scale drawing is preferable, with all the components drawn in place. Once the basic principles of whirligig design—as described here—are known, they can be applied to many forms and shapes. The detailed drawings are of working models, and the steps in their construction should be studied carefully before a person starts to make them.

Anyone considering developing an original model should keep in mind that there is something special about a whirligig. People like them not just because they are wind machines, although that is interesting in itself. The best ones fascinate us because they are droll, whimsical, humorous, unusual, startling, and aesthetic. They are rhythmical and graceful in motion. Because of the beauty of their design and movement, and their artistic integrity, a few belong to the category of kinetic sculpture. Perhaps you can create one of these, but remember, *design comes first!*

CONSTRUCTION

General instructions for building whirligigs are provided with this book, with the basic principles of construction discussed in Chapter 3. Specific instructions for each of several different whirligigs are provided, with technical drawings, in Chapters 4 through 7. The instructions are easy to follow, and the whirligigs will work if they are constructed according to the directions. A few matters relative to construction are considered here.

Materials

The most wonderful thing about whirligigs, apart from the fact that they are fun to create and fabricate, is that they are inexpensive to build. A few scraps of wood, a couple of tools, and a nail or two are all that are needed. Most homes have some boards around the house, some tools, and an assortment of screws and nails. The whirligigs in this book call for some special-sized screws and washers, and some small tubing—all inexpensive—but even these are not absolutely necessary. Substitutes can be made in some cases and some items done without. Of course, if one has access to a number of tools and a selection of materials, so much the better.

Basic Tools

Only a few tools are required. These are (1) saws: coping, compass, or band saw for wood, a hacksaw for nails, and a smaller saw that will cut through metal tubing; (2) drill and selected bits: a hand drill (adequate and may be preferred), or an electric drill; (3) woodcarving knives, or a pocket knife; (4) wire-cutting pliers; (5) tin shears: for cutting metal propellers; (6) hammer; (7) screwdriver; (8) wood file or rasp; and (9) sandpaper.

Wood

Most of the whirligig bodies and frames described in the text can be made of any available 1″ lumber (milled to ¾″). The flat figures are made of various grades of pine lumber. The carved figures in the round can be cut from almost any leftover 2 × 4 without any knots in it, but a clear soft wood, easy to carve, like white pine, is preferable.

Mounting Stand

A simple stand for holding a whirligig while it's being completed is suggested. Such a mount will hold the body in its proper position and make it easier to work on. It will also protect the propellers and other appurtenances when they are attached. The size of the stand needed depends on the size of the whirligig. It is better to have too large a stand than one too small.

Stands for the whirligigs in this book are shown in Fig. 1.3. They are for guidance only, and the builder should feel free to model any stand that will work. Stand A has a base of $\frac{1}{4}$" plywood which measures 4" × 5" and a post which measures $1\frac{1}{2}$" × $1\frac{1}{2}$" × 5". This is high enough to permit wing propellers to turn and the witch's broom to clear the base. Stand B has a 5" piece of old broomstick set into a base measuring $\frac{3}{4}$" × 6" × 6". A 10-penny nail with the head cut off is driven into the top of each post to serve as a pivot pin or spindle. A heavy mechanical whirligig needs a larger working stand. Stand C is 2" thick and 8" square. It has a headless 30-penny nail driven into the center of one face for a pivot pin.

If the whirligig is to be on exhibit, a finished and stained – or painted – mounting stand should be constructed. It should be kept dignified and simple. My arm-waving whirligigs stand on a nail driven up through a $\frac{3}{4}$" piece of wood 4" square, stained and varnished. The birds need more wing room, so I add posts to the stands for these whirligigs.

Fan

A fan is not essential, but it is most helpful in the testing process. It need not be very large or forceful but should be big enough to create a steady flow of air around the whirligig. When one is trying out a new design or making sure that the whirligig works, having a fan on hand is better than waiting for the wind to blow.

Labeling Parts

It is sometimes advisable to label each piece as you work. For example, in carving an Indian paddling a canoe, I found it necessary to label the arms "left inside" and "right inside" because I was trying to continue the carving of the shoulders (paddle bases) into the paddles. With birds' wings it is essential that you label the matched pairs. Tagging the pieces will avoid confusion, mismatching, and other er-

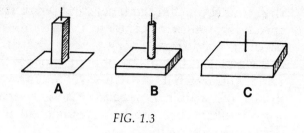

FIG. 1.3

rors, particularly if you find yourself working on several whirligigs at one time.

Drafting and Copying

Drawing a design on regular graph paper sometimes simplifies the work. It is subsequently easier to stylize the drawing and make measurements to scale. Drawings can also be reduced or enlarged by means of squared paper. There are several types of graph paper, the most useful types of which have either 4 spaces to the inch, or 8 spaces to the inch.

But, of course, when an idea strikes, any scrap of paper will do, at least for the moment! Once the design is drawn to full scale (or is available, as many in this book are), it is advisable to trace the design on cardboard and cut out a cardboard pattern or series of patterns. These are used to trace the outline on wood blocks. They have another advantage: Patterns may be used over again.

Putting It All Together

As to the whole pattern of work, you will soon establish a routine so that you will begin first things first and then go on from there. Let me explain by describing a recent experience. The Country Store in Chapel Hill, North Carolina, telephoned to say that a customer wanted a whirligig of a man rowing a boat. Assuming that a large mechanical whirligig was not called for, I sat down with paper and pencil and made a quick sketch of a rowboat 12" long. I located the centerline and added a crude figure straining at the oars. I located the hub point at the man's shoulders and a pivot point on the boat. The oars that I drew proved to be about 5" long. With a ruler I measured off the

4

sketch and straightened out the lines. The man's body was formalized. I traced the boat, oarsman, and oars separately on cardboard and cut out patterns. These were transferred to boards and sawed out. A pivot socket was drilled into the boat's bottom. Shoulder blocks were glued to the figure, and a hole was drilled through for the axle. Then the figure was glued to the boat. I cut out the oars and shaped them like two parts of a single propeller. They were drilled and attached to a small brass rod through the body. I placed the unfinished whirligig on a mounting stand and turned on the fan. The boat swung sideways to the breeze, and the man began to row furiously. The whirligig was a success, and it could now be finished and painted. (Plans and instructions for Man Rowing Boat are provided in Chapter 5.)

That was the design and work cycle for an idea new to me. You will be able to do the same thing with almost any idea after you have learned what is involved in putting it all together. The first step is to decide what type of whirligig you're interested in building.

A final word: My principal purpose in creating this book is to interest people in whirligigs and to encourage them to have fun making them. The book contains patterns and instructions for making 30 whirligigs, all of which are designed to work outdoors in the wind. They are not difficult to make, and anyone who wants to make these particular whirligigs needs only to follow the directions. The reader may already have noted, however, that I have another purpose in mind. It is to encourage people to create new designs and make whirligigs which reflect the individuality of the maker. This is how many of the independent whirligig makers of the past centuries worked. Once they caught on to the simple technical aspects of whirligig construction, they used their imaginations and ingenuity to make new models. Creating new whirligigs is fun, and seeing them finally spin and twirl in the wind is very exciting and rewarding.

2

Types of Whirligigs

There are innumerable whirligig designs, and every craftsperson sooner or later develops his or her own individual designs, which become part of the tradition of whirligig creation. There are certain basic construction principles, and once these are learned, they can be used to build whirligigs of every description. Four basic types of whirligigs are discussed in this section: winged, arm-waving, weathervane and special kinds, and mechanical. Their design and construction are described, and examples of each type are provided in drawings which are, in most instances, of exact working size.

WINGED WHIRLIGIGS

The principle of the winged type is two similar and balanced propellers, rotating in opposite directions (Fig. 2.1). This provides balance to the body and creates a realistic, flashing-wing effect. Whirligig wings can be used with nearly any object as the body. Included in this book is a drawing of a dragon whirligig, which is very popular with children. Remember, wings can be put on almost anything, not just on angels!

Most winged whirligigs are birds, however, and those illustrated in this book are the

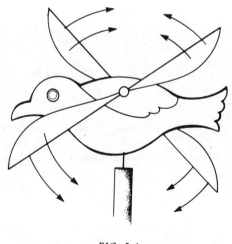

FIG. 2.1

American Goldfinch, the Eastern Bluebird, the Robin, and the Cardinal. Using the same basic design, the craftsperson can make whirligigs of any species of bird, real or imaginary. A bird may be sketched from life or traced from a bird guide, and the drawing transferred to ordinary one-inch board (milled to ¾"). While size is up to the maker, I recommend that bird whirligigs be made life-sized. This adds a sense of reality and also makes it proportionally correct when placed among models of other species. The American Goldfinch is about 5" long in life, while the seagull is 24" in length. In my yard, the little goldfinch whirls its wings rapidly while the big seagull flaps its wings slowly and majestically. Both models look just right and seem ready to take off.

Two-winged whirligigs are balanced so that the wind catches them and holds them slightly angled or sideways to the wind. This makes the propellers move. If for some reason the whirligig is unbalanced, and faces directly into the wind or away from it, the relationship of the pivot point to the hub position should be studied. Adjustment of the pivot location is probably all that is needed. Malfunctions in winged types seldom occur, and most problems are caused by errors which can be quickly remedied.

The basic concept of the winged whirligig has been used successfully for other wind toys in which the propellers have no resemblance to wings. Modern Times (see Fig. 4.11) is a modernistic creation in which the "wings" are simply moving objects.

ARM-WAVING WHIRLIGIGS

No one knows who made the first arm-waving whirligigs that became popular in the early 19th century. They were designed to operate entirely by balance, and the relationship of the pivot to the hub was all-important. The arms rotated in the wind while the body twisted and turned. As one observer put it, "They whirl and gig at the same time!" In this reference are found the origins of the word *whirligig*. Both *whirl* and *gig* signify *turn* in Old English and seem to be derived from words of

that meaning in Old Norse. To many experts, the early arm-waving, twisting and turning figure is the true whirligig.

There is evidence that during the 19th century some designs were mass-produced and sold throughout the country. Popular types were easily identified characters, such as uniformed soldiers waving swords or sailors waving signal flags (Fig. 2.2). General George Washington astride his horse and brandishing his sword was a familiar subject.

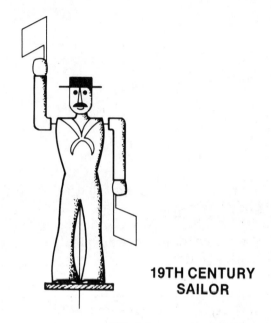

19TH CENTURY SAILOR

FIG. 2.2

The two arms constitute the blades of a simple propeller, and the propeller principle of opposing slanted blades must be kept in mind during design and construction. One arm must be angled one way, and the other the other way. The arms are joined at the hub to an axle made of a metal rod or wood dowel, which passes at right angles through the body. In carving the arms, care must be taken to keep the arms away from the body so they may spin without interference. The arms must be trimmed down as much as possible to keep them lightweight.

To function properly, the hub (H) and pivot (P) must be in a correct relationship to each

7

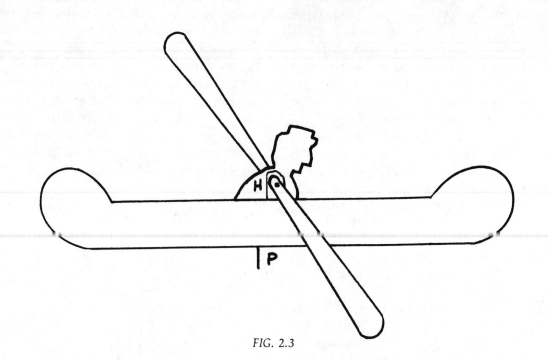

FIG. 2.3

other (Fig. 2.3). In upright figures, the hub is slightly forward of the centerline and the pivot slightly behind it. This relationship will be discussed at length in the section that details construction of arm-waving whirligigs.

Sometimes it's advisable, because of the shape or design of the figure, to add a tail assembly. A rudder will guarantee that the whirligig will always get the most out of any breeze by causing the whirligig to turn its propeller arms into the wind. A tail assembly also provides an opportunity to have some fun with the shape of the rudder. For instance, a soldier can have a gravestone, a walking gentleman a milestone, and a dog a fire hydrant.

I developed the tail assembly idea when one of the antiques I copied simply did not work, and I wondered how I could make it operative. There are many ways to make a whirligig face in a certain direction to the wind, such as using fins, vanes, rudders, and the like, and an inventive person can find hours of enjoyment solving such problems.

The subject matter for the arm-waving type is endless. Sports fans can make baseball pitchers forever warming up and football players endlessly passing. There are the traditional

8

bathing beauties waving colorful towels, but female figures today need have no limit to their activities. The arm-waving whirligig type is not restricted to humans. For a goat owner, I made a Nubian goat waving its big ears (plans are provided in Chapter 4).

In the 1930s, a familiar sight along roadsides was the figure of an Indian paddling a canoe. This remains one of the easiest whirligigs to make, which may account for its popularity. Its construction is discussed in Chapter 5.

WEATHERVANE WHIRLIGIGS AND OTHER SPECIAL TYPES

A vane is a rotating device that shows the direction of the wind, and the word stems from an Old English word for *banner*. There are two elements in a weathervane: the body and the pivot. To locate the pivot, first find the center of balance (B) of the body, then locate the pivot point (P) forward of B (Fig. 2.4). The proper distance is a matter of judgment. The weathervane should move easily with wind changes and always point into the wind.

The weathervane whirligig is built like a

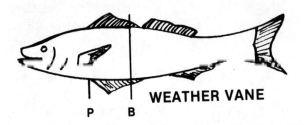

WEATHER VANE

P   B

FIG. 2.4

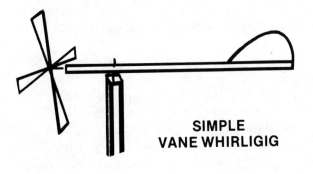

**SIMPLE
VANE WHIRLIGIG**

FIG. 2.5

vane; it acts like one, too, with the addition of one or more propellers that whirl around, providing the action (Fig. 2.5). The simplest type can be made in a few moments, and I have several going in my yard to test propellers and just to enjoy.

Willy the Whale and the Flying Witch in Chapter 6 are examples of weathervane whirligigs. Willy has a simple two-bladed propeller on his nose, and the Witch has a multibladed propeller on the end of her broomstick. Ships with twirling propellers at their sterns are well-known whirligigs, and a submarine and an ocean liner are included among the working weathervane models.

While weathervane whirligigs face into the wind and show which way it's blowing, some other types seem to have no function other than to be decorative. The only movement is that provided by propellers. They are still called "whirligigs."

Propellers of every conceivable design have been placed everywhere on objects. A number of interesting possibilities are illustrated in Fig. 2.6. Propellers have served as automobile

wheels, aircraft propellers, ferris wheels, ship propellers, carriage wheels, bicycles, non-objective mobiles, and just about anything utilizing rotary motion.

There are many special decorative uses, and there is always the question of when a wind toy ceases to be a whirligig. Still, if a primitive pinwheel is considered to be one, practically in a class by itself, then any whirling fun object moved by the wind can apply for membership in the whirligig class.

MECHANICAL WHIRLIGIGS

Because it's a mechanism for utilizing and applying wind power, the mechanical whirli-

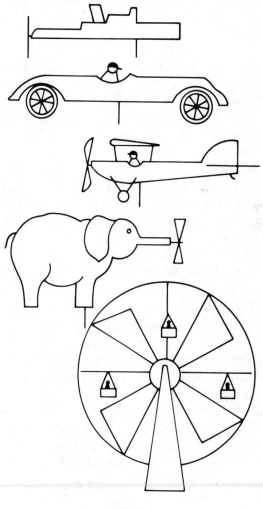

FIG. 2.6

FIG. 2.7

as large as four feet in diameter, are still being made in the Appalachians, but most of those popularly constructed are relatively small and easy to handle. The Churning Woman, illustrated in Chapter 7, is an adaptation of one made in North Carolina. The frame measures 10" × 13", and it has an additional 5" rudder or tail. The four-bladed propeller is 15" in diameter. In a high wind, the churning is frantic and funny, but if the wind is too strong the yoke breaks, and the rod bends. However, as a machine to watch on days when there is a light, steady breeze, it can't be beat. The motion has a rhythmic, soothing quality, even though the woman's toil goes on forever.

As with other whirligigs, making a complex mechanical one is an inexpensive proposition. It is the idea that counts, and ideas are free. Most makers of mechanical whirligigs take what they have at hand and use it. The first mechanical model I studied had a curtain rod for a sleeve, an old, rusty bolt for a drive shaft, and a wheel from a child's toy for a gear. On another, the propellers were made of leftover cedar shingles. These were of perfect weight, did not require painting, and were easy to fashion.

Building a new mechanical whirligig usually takes some time. The work will be made easier if a detailed design is prepared first. Even then, adjustments and changes will undoubtedly be necessary. Half the fun lies in solving the many engineering problems which are inevitable with these fascinating whirligigs.

The characteristics of the various types (winged, arm-waving, weathervane, and mechanical) have been combined in one way or another to create original and quite unusual whirligigs (Fig. 2.8). Some of these have been large devices for show or exhibition. Others have been of modest size. Every whirligig builder has an opportunity to demonstrate his or her cleverness in combining the traits of the various types. There is no restriction on size or design, so long as what results is a true whirligig: It is powered by the wind, and it is planned for fun.

gig is a machine. By some definitions it might also be called an engine, since it converts wind energy into mechanical power. Using cams, gears, or wheels, this type of whirligig changes the rotary motion of the propeller into vertical or horizontal movement, which then makes figures and objects move by means of connecting rods or wires (see Fig. 2.7). Usually the objects and their motion are designed to be humorous. Often they reflect frontier or rural American culture: a woman endlessly churning butter or washing clothes in a tub, a man forever sawing or chopping wood, or continuously pedaling a bicycle, a mule repeatedly kicking up its heels (often at a farmer). Inventive minds have elaborated on these ideas, and some whirligigs have several activities going on at once. They are so complicated that months of time must have been devoted to planning them.

The mechanical whirligig is usually larger and heavier than other types and requires a strong frame, metal parts, and a sturdy pivot. Some relatively huge models, with propellers

FIG. 2.8

3

Basic Whirligig Parts

All whirligigs—no matter what type—have several basic elements in common, and no matter how complicated a whirligig may seem, its mechanism may be analyzed in terms of these essentials (Fig. 3.1).

BODY

The body of the whirligig is the human figure, the bird, or whatever other form is used. The bodies in this booklet are made of wood. The flat bodies are standard one-inch pine (milled $\frac{3}{4}$"), and the round figures are made of thicker pieces, up to $2\frac{1}{4}$".

WING BASE

The wing base is designed to keep the propeller away from the body of the whirligig. It may be made in any appropriate size. The goldfinch has a small wing base: $\frac{1}{2}$" × $\frac{1}{2}$" × $\frac{3}{4}$". A seagull has a much larger base: $\frac{3}{4}$" ×

$2\frac{1}{2}$" × 5". A pilot hole is usually drilled in the middle to accommodate the screw which will go through the hub of the propeller into the wing base (Fig. 3.2).

PIVOT

Each whirligig is balanced on, and turns around, its pivot point. For this to occur, a hole is drilled in the base of the whirligig, making a socket on which it rides on a rod or spindle. To make the whirligig function effectively, and also to prolong its operating life, the socket is lined with a metal sleeve and has a piece of metal at its base. The socket liner is made of brass, steel, or aluminum tubing or similar cylinders, such as tension pins. The metal piece, or cap, at the base can be part of a cutoff nail of the proper diameter. This serves as a bearing for the pivot spindle. In addition to the nail piece, or in its place, a ball bearing or steel BB may be used.

The spindle can be a headless nail or a steel

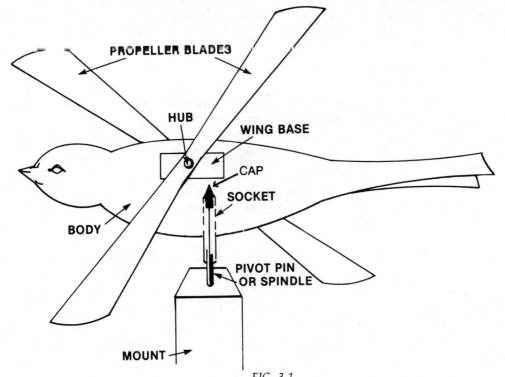

FIG. 3.1

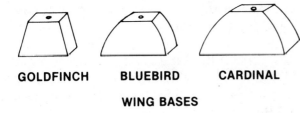

GOLDFINCH   BLUEBIRD   CARDINAL

WING BASES

FIG. 3.2

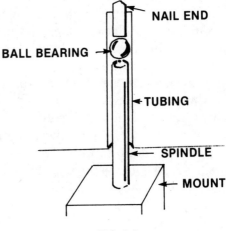

FIG. 3.3

rod of the right size set in a pole, stick, or dowel. The pole should be small enough in diameter to permit the free movement of the arms or wings and may be nailed to a fence post or other larger support. The pivot mechanism is illustrated in Fig. 3.3.

Tubing sizes for socket liners shown in this book are $\frac{1}{16}$", $\frac{7}{32}$", and $\frac{1}{4}$". Tension pins in 1" and 2" lengths may also be used. Pivot pins or spindles to fit the tubing are 10-penny, 16-penny, and 30-penny nails, respectively. Metal rods which fit the socket liners may also be used. Nails or rods must not have too close a fit, as freedom of movement is essential to a

whirligig. Suggested sizes of these materials are included in each section on construction.

PROPELLER

A propeller may be defined as a rotating device with a central hub and radiating blades

13

set at an angle to provide a very steep pitch. If we say that all whirligigs are driven by propellers modified in one way or another, we will not be far from right. The earliest whirligig was probably a simple pinwheel, or something of the sort, that was little more than a propeller. There are two basic types of whirligigs according to their use of the propeller: nonmechanical and mechanical. On nonmechanical whirligigs, the propellers merely put on a show by twirling. The mechanical whirligig uses a propeller as a means of harnessing wind power to make other things move. There are four main types of propellers conventionally used in whirligigs.

Basic Style

The most familiar propeller has two blades opposite each other and is evenly balanced at the center, or hub. Construction of a propeller with a woodcarving knife is relatively simple, as long as one remembers that the propeller blades must be set at opposite angles so, when held at the hub, the blades traveling in a circle attack the air at the same angle.

The example that follows relates to the construction of a wing for the Cardinal whirligig. The wood block measures $\frac{3}{4}'' \times 1'' \times 8''$ and, though the size will be different for other models, the procedure is the same for all the bird wings for whirligigs in this book.

To construct the basic propeller, begin by marking off the block as indicated, marking the ends, also, so you will not forget the different angles of the blades (Fig. 3.4).

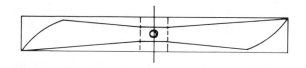

FIG. 3.4

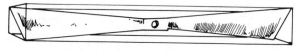

FIG. 3.5

Next, drill the center hole, or hub (Fig. 3.5). For the basic propellers in this book, the hub will be fitted with a $\frac{3}{16}''$ metal sleeve, and a $1\frac{1}{4}''$ No. 6 roundhead screw will serve as the axle.

Then cut out the basic form, and proceed to shape and smooth the blades, using knives, a file, and sandpaper.

The aim is to make the propeller as light as possible without jeopardizing its functional strength. Maintaining the width of the blades is crucial, also, as this feature is important for harnessing the wind. Whirligig makers are urged to use their ingenuity to make propellers as efficient and graceful as possible. Hubs can be narrowed to reduce weight, and wings can be made more shapely. When the propeller is finished, spin it at the hub. If it is not balanced, the same blade will be at the bottom each time the rotation stops. Cut or sand it until it is balanced. Propellers—especially large ones—must be balanced for efficient movement.

Modified Propellers

An example of the modified propeller is an old-fashioned whirligig's waving arms, which constitute propeller blades. They are sometimes difficult to shape efficiently because, in addition to resembling arms, they must carry swords, flags, or other objects. Nevertheless, everything should be done to keep them thin, while maintaining a good propeller angle and wide blades.

As with the basic propeller, the arms are drawn on a wood block and cut out as shown. Holding the arm to the whirligig body, the angle at which each one should be cut can be determined, and the angle should be drawn on the end of the block. At the same time, the location of the axle should be checked on the body and the arm blocks. In effect, the two arms are the blades of one propeller, joined by an axle at H, as shown in Fig. 3.6.

If the body is three-dimensional, it is best to drill the hole for the axle before the body is carved. This makes drilling easier. The size of the hole through the body depends on the size of the axle and its sleeve. The sleeve is placed

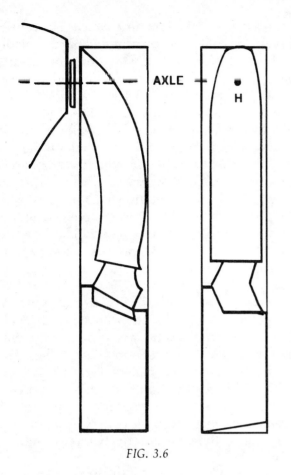

FIG. 3.6

in the body first, then the rod or axle is tested for size and fit.

Smaller holes are drilled into the arms and, at the last stages of construction, the arms—filled with adhesive material—are pressed into the axle, or screwed on if the axle ends are threaded. If the axle turns freely in the sleeve or bearing, the balanced arms will need no further work. Danger to such arms rarely comes from the wind, but they are sometimes broken by people who feel they must turn the arms with their fingers. Arm-spinners should be advised to imitate the wind and blow on them.

An exception to the modified propeller should be noted here. Some museum whirligig models have paddle arms that are not angled, as propellers are. They are set at right angles to each other. When tested, they operate jerkily on a center pivot but without sustained movement. Such propellers and any other oddly shaped turning device that attracts your eye should be tested for movement before you

get too deeply into problems that have no immediate or easy solution.

The modified propeller can be used for purposes other than arms for a human figure, although these have been most common in the past. Doggie, the model illustrated in Chapter 5, waves his paws, and the Nubian goat mentioned earlier twirls its ears. The modified type can also be used with creative, abstract models. When designing new whirligigs using modified propellers, one must be careful not to construct a body of such size and shape that it will hide the propellers from the wind. If the propellers do not have access to a free flow of air, the whirligig will not work well, if at all.

Multibladed Designs

Multibladed propellers may be small or large. They are used for humorous and decorative purposes in some whirligigs, and as a source of wind power on others. The basic construction is shown in Fig. 3.7. Blades of any shape are cut with a stub. The hub is drilled to take the stub, and the blades are set at an angle. Multibladed propellers are usually very efficient.

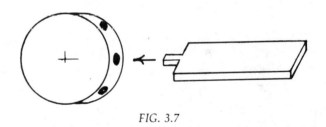

FIG. 3.7

The same type of construction, or a modification of it, can be used to make propellers of any size and design, and one needs only to consider windmills to see how big they can become. Incidentally, small windmill models make superior whirligigs. These have been around a long time, perhaps longer than we know. The windmill was probably invented in ancient China, passed slowly through the Middle East, and was brought to Europe by the Arabs before the 12th century. In addition to the arms and sails of windmills, there are as many multibladed designs for whirligigs as

15

you can imagine (four possibilities are shown in Figs. 3.8 and 3.9).

Metal Propellers

Various types of propellers can be made out of sheet metal. An excellent lightweight metal is aluminum flashing material, which comes in small rolls, or in small pieces (5″ × 7″) readily usable for whirligig parts. The aluminum flashing serves well for small, independent propellers, as used on ship weathervane types, and for blades of propellers on large models. Such lightweight material is easily bent, however, and for some whirligigs a heavier metal, such as galvanized steel, may be required.

Propeller designs are drawn on the metal

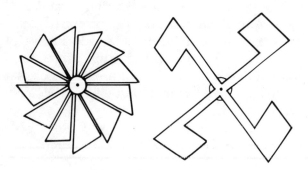

FIG. 3.8

with a glass marker or china pencil. The center holes are drilled or punched, and the blade outlines are cut with tinsnips or a metal-cutting saw (see examples of ship and turbine types in Figs. 3.10 and 3.11). Then the blades are turned—each in the same direction—usually by hand and, if necessary, with the aid of pliers. Large, independent metal propellers and those that will be used on driveshafts can be cut in the same manner.

Metal propellers require hubs of some sort to hold them steady. They can be fastened to their driveshafts in various ways. They may be held by nuts and lock washers, as shown in Fig. 3.12, or they may be soldered or welded in place.

Few whirligig makers will construct a power propeller entirely of metal. Most such propellers have a wooden hub and arms, with metal blades added. The reason for this may be artistic. While turbine propellers, for example, are more efficient, they can't compare in appearance with handmade wooden propellers of creative design. Metal propellers may not permit the individual creativity many people want.

One word of warning: Cut metal edges are sharp, and care should be taken when working with metal propellers. Wear gloves. Also, remember that large metal propellers turning rapidly in a high wind can be dangerous.

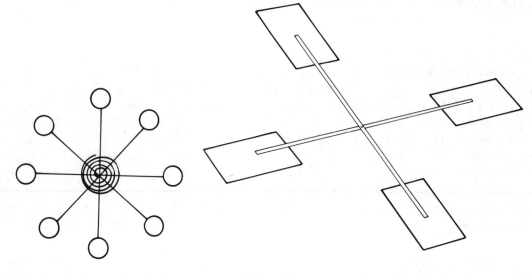

FIG. 3.9

Mechanical Styles

The mechanical type of whirligig requires a large, power-producing propeller. It must harness the wind's energy and, by means of a driveshaft, power train, or camshaft, make other things move. Typical working propellers are those used on the mechanical whirligigs in Chapter 7. The one for the Churning Woman is 15″ in diameter and that for the Signaling Trainman is 12″ in diameter. Much larger propellers have been used, and some mechanical types are described as having drivers 4 feet in diameter. I have an antique homemade frame with arms of old broomsticks, with blade-holders attached, which has a radius of 25½″. The hub has an aperture for a ½″ shaft. While, in theory, there is no limit to the size of a whirligig propeller, there is a point where the mechanism becomes something more than a whirligig. That point, apparently, has not really been defined.

The large propellers described in Chapter 7 have a wooden hub and metal blades. Such propellers may be made entirely of metal, but they may also be made completely of wood. One such propeller is illustrated in Fig. 3.13, shown about one-quarter size. The rough-cut blades are 10″ long, 4″ wide, and ½″ thick. The hub is 3″ square and 2″ thick. It is a homemade product, and the individuality of the designer is indicated throughout, especially in the shape of the blades. The wood is unpainted, and the workmanship quite crude. But the relatively heavy propeller operates perfectly.

In constructing new mechanical whirligigs, one must keep in mind that the projected size of the propeller should depend upon the power required to activate the whirligig. The general rule is to design the smallest propeller that will do the job. Never underestimate the pow-

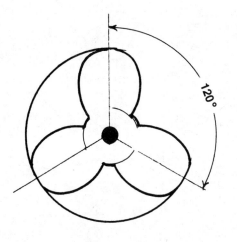

SHIP TYPE

FIG. 3.10

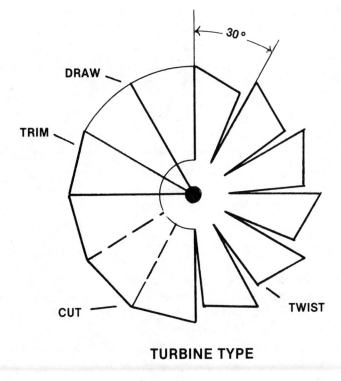

TURBINE TYPE

FIG. 3.11

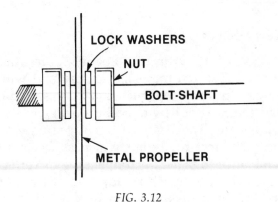

FIG. 3.12

17

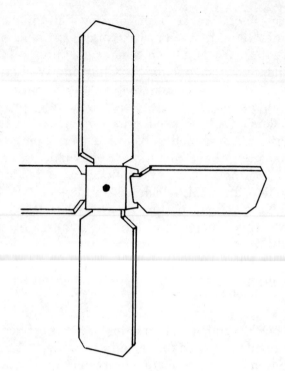

FIG. 3.13

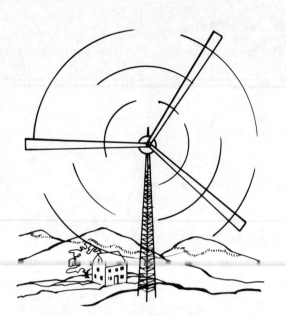

FIG. 3.14

FIG. 3.15

er of the wind. Too large a propeller can tear a mechanism apart.

The 12″ and 15″ propellers described in Chapter 7 should activate simple mechanisms, even larger whirligigs than those for which they were designed.

The selection of a propeller for a new whirligig is largely a matter of choice and individual preference. There are factors other than sheer size to be taken into account. The width of the blades and their weight make a difference. Other things being equal, width increases speed and force, and weight adds a certain ponderousness and inertia to the movement.

New Designs

Recent interest in new energy sources has revived research into solar energy and wind power. In many countries this has resulted in development of new radical propeller and rotor designs. These range from huge rotary devices 200 feet high—but which still bear resemblance to standard propellers—to vertical vane machines which are adjusted by computers. Whirligig makers are encouraged to study

18

these devices. Some will provide ways to more efficiently power various mechanical whirligigs, while others will undoubtedly lead to new whirligig designs.

A person who has the inclination can make scale models of the new propellers and test them. Illustrations of these devices abound in the many books that have been published re-

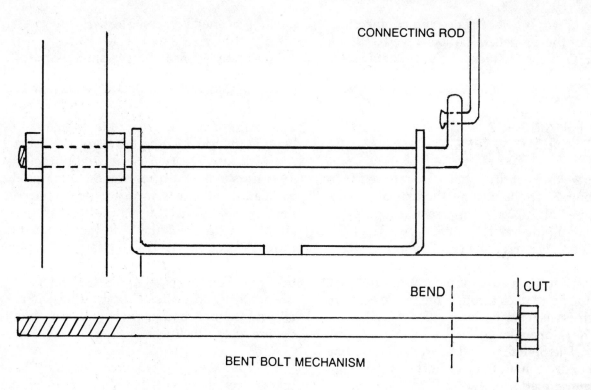

CONNECTING ROD

BEND | | CUT

BENT BOLT MECHANISM

FIG. 3.16

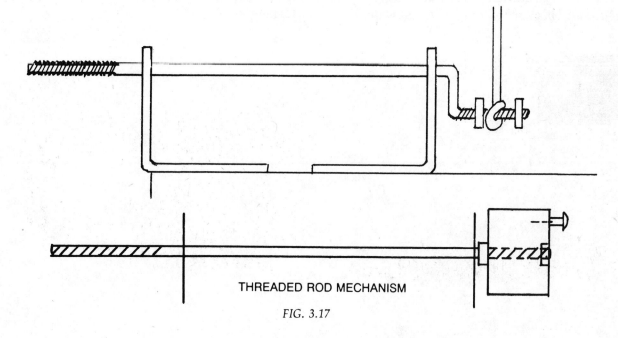

THREADED ROD MECHANISM

FIG. 3.17

19

lating to windpower science and engineering. Most of the propellers can be copied and will work. One can even try one's hand at inventing a new propeller!

DRIVESHAFTS FOR MECHANICAL WHIRLIGIGS

Three kinds of driveshafts are referred to in Chapter 7. The Churning Woman uses a $\frac{1}{4}$" carriage bolt, 6" long. It passes through a $\frac{5}{16}$" piece of tubing in a $1\frac{1}{2}$" square post. The head of the bolt is embedded securely in a 2" wheel to which a connecting wire is attached, providing an up-and-down movement. The threaded end goes through the propeller hub, which is secured on both sides by $\frac{1}{4}$" nuts. Washers are placed between the moving parts. The Signaling Trainman uses the same kind of driveshaft, but transfers its movement above the platform.

Bolts of various sizes can be used in several ways. For example, the head of a bolt can be cut off, the end bent over $\frac{3}{4}$", and filed flat. A hole is drilled through the flat part and a connecting rod is attached to it. The bolt is held in position by metal braces. The bent bolt mechanism is shown in Fig. 3.16.

The threaded rod shaft is simple and efficient (Fig. 3.17). A $\frac{1}{8}$" metal rod, $6\frac{1}{2}$" long, is threaded with a 6/32 die for a distance of 1" at the front (propeller) end and $\frac{3}{4}$" at the back end. At 1" from the rear, put a right-angle bend in the rod and another bend at $\frac{1}{2}$". Place the rod between two right-angle brackets. Two nuts hold the propeller in place at the front and, at the rear, form a place for the connecting rod. Threading $\frac{1}{8}$" rods is relatively simple. Inexpensive dies and handles can be purchased at any hardware store, which can also supply nuts, washers, and angle iron brackets. Rods are available at stores that handle welding supplies. Maybe there is one around the house; most heavy drapery hangers are of $\frac{1}{8}$" thickness.

The following construction sections (Chapters 4 through 7) are divided into five parts: a brief introduction, basic steps in designing a whirligig, notes on construction with special details on sample models, a summary of material sizes, and full-scale drawings of working whirligigs.

4

Construction of
Winged Whirligigs

All winged whirligigs must "fly" sideways to the wind in order that the wing / propellers are at right angles to the flow of air. This requires establishing the proper relationship between the pivot point and the hub point. This relationship and the basic parts of a winged whirligig have been described in Chapter 3.

This section deals with the details of construction of three different winged types: the standard bird whirligig with two separate wings (American Goldfinch, Bluebird, Cardinal, Robin, and Danny the Dragon); the split-wing whirligig (Puffin and Pegasus) and a variety, Nanny the Goat; and the modified-wing type (Modern Times). After becoming familiar with these types, the craftsperson should have little difficulty designing other winged models.

BASIC STEPS

This section will explain the construction of the winged models in this chapter, as well as instruct those who wish to create their own models.

Design

The first step is to plan the design. If you are interested in a particular bird, you can find a drawing or photo in a bird guide. Draw it full-size on graph paper. Plan the wings, which should extend beyond the body. Locate the tentative pivot hole (P) and hub (H). Sketch a wing base for the model. Check your pattern against those provided in the book and make similar patterns of the body profile and wing outline.

Body

After the design has been selected, trace or draw the outline of the body on the wood block and cut it out with a saw. File down the rough spots and sand it well. Cut out the wing bases and sand them also, then drill a small hole (¼" or so) in the center of the block for the axle. Find the balance point (B) of the body by balancing it on a narrow object such as a pencil. Locate the pivot point (P) $\frac{1}{4}$" behind the balance point. This will be drilled for the pivot socket. At a distance $\frac{1}{4}$" before B, place a mark. From that mark, draw a vertical line up the side of the body. On the line, near the top of the body—or at another appropriate place, depending on the whirligig—is located the hub point (H), where the center of the wing block and the wing/propeller will be located.

For the pivot socket, drill a hole one inch deep (or more, depending upon the size of the body) up into the body to receive the socket liner. Into the socket, hammer a piece of metal (such as a piece of nail) to act as a bearing. Later, a ball bearing may also be added.

Wing Base

The wing base is located along the vertical line that established the hub's position and is securely glued in place with water-resistant glue. With large birds or objects, wire brads or small nails should be driven through for additional strength. It is advisable to drill small holes where the nails will be inserted to prevent the wood from splitting. The hole in the block should fit over the established hub point. Check the bird diagram in Fig. 3.1 to see how it all fits together.

Wings

As indicated, the two wings must be cut to run opposite each other, spinning in different directions. They should be carved in pairs, be of the same size, and balanced. They need not be of the exact same weight. The hub of each propeller is drilled and fitted with a $\frac{3}{16}$" metal sleeve.

The easiest way to attach the wings so they will fly correctly is to view them from the front of the bird or figure. Hold them so the blades show a V formation, as seen in Fig. 4.1. (From the back, they will have a reverse—or upside down V—pattern.) The propellers must be designed and cut this way for each bird or object. This assures that they will turn opposite each other, spinning in different directions in the

22

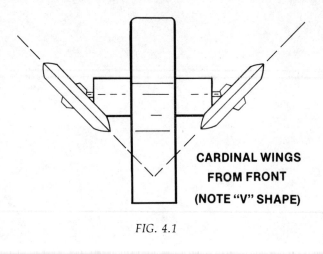

CARDINAL WINGS
FROM FRONT
(NOTE "V" SHAPE)

FIG. 4.1

wind, one clockwise and the other counterclockwise.

If, for some reason, the propellers happen to be cut exactly the same, do not despair. This kind of thing happens to all of us sooner or later, and the solution is simple. Make two more with their blades angled the opposite way, and you will end up with two sets of wings.

The propellers are mounted with No. 6 brass roundheaded screws, $1\frac{1}{4}$" long, with two No. 6 brass washers on each axle (Fig.

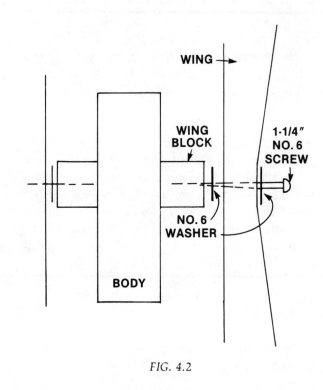

FIG. 4.2

4.2). Brass is not absolutely necessary, but it weathers well. The wings should move freely. Weather may cause the wood to swell and tighten all the parts. If so, the screws can be loosened. Or the screws may become loose in the wood and can be made secure with the addition of water-resistant glue. In difficult cases, wood filler and one of the epoxy wonder glues will prove useful.

Assembly

It's best that the body and wings be painted separately, before the wings are attached to the body. The mounting stand will hold the body for the painting task. For painting the wings, a different kind of stand is suggested. This is primarily an upright post, with small nails projecting from the sides, as shown in Fig. 4.3.

WING PAINTING STAND

FIG. 4.3

If the whirligig is to be decorative and exhibited indoors, any kind of paint—including watercolors—can be used. If a working outdoor whirligig is intended, it should be painted with a preservative and waterproof exterior paint.

The pivot pin or spindle may be any rod that fits the socket. A nail with the head cut off and filed smooth and round makes an excellent spindle. A steel BB or ball bearing placed between the pivot pin and the socket base will allow the whirligig to rotate freely.

STANDARD BIRD MODELS

The four garden birds—American Goldfinch, Eastern Bluebird (Fig. 4.5), Robin, and Cardinal—are constructed along standard whirligig lines. They are small and relatively easy to make. If the propellers are light and well-balanced, they will fly cheerfully in any breeze. Danny the Dragon, a variety of the winged type, has a more vertical body than a bird (see Fig. 4.4). Nevertheless, he flaps his wings nicely and is a harmless and happy dragon. Detailed instructions are given below for construction of the Cardinal to show how the regular smaller bird whirligigs are made.

The Cardinal

MATERIALS
Body block: $\frac{3}{4}$" × 3" × $8\frac{1}{2}$"
Wing base (2): $\frac{5}{8}$" × $\frac{5}{8}$" × $1\frac{1}{4}$"
Wings: $\frac{3}{4}$" × 1" × 8"
Wing sleeves: $\frac{3}{16}$" brass tubing (or nothing)

FIG. 4.4

23

Axle: 1¼" brass roundheaded No. 6 screw
Socket liner: ⁷⁄₃₂" brass tubing
Pivot pin: 16d nail, or rod

CONSTRUCTION

1. Trace the body pattern on wood, marking the hub (H) and pivot point (P). Cut it out and drill the ⁷⁄₃₂" socket hole, about 1" deep. Insert the socket liner, if one is

FIG. 4.5

used. Place a cap at the base of the socket; this can be the end of a cut-off 16d nail, or small roundheaded screw. Sand the bird well, rounding off the edges. Mark out the color lines around the head.

2. Cut out the wing bases. In the center,

drill small pilot holes for the hub screws. Sand them and glue them in place, using clamps, with the hub holes in the H position. They may be further reinforced with wire brads.

3. Cut out the wings, making sure each will turn in a different direction. This is very important: each must balance. Drill the hubs with a ³⁄₁₆" bit and insert brass tubing (or nothing) to act as sleeves. When finished, you will have two propellers; each will turn in a reverse direction to the other.

4. Paint the body and wings separately. If the whirligig is to be used outside, a coat of waterproof sealer may be applied first. Two coats of oil paint will last a long time. If it is to be kept inside, any paint will do. Incidentally, some people treat their whirligig as a pet and bring it indoors in inclement weather.

5. Attach the wings with No. 6 roundheaded screws and washers. Place the cardinal on a mounting or post with a 16d nail, with head cut off, as a spindle, and watch it fly!

The other birds in this book are constructed in the same way. The same design principles will apply to all other birds, even larger models. Simply draw the bird full size (the Seagull and the Mallard Duck are about 24" long in life) and transfer the pattern to the wood. The larger birds will require larger wing bases and longer wings (about 22" for the Mallard). Such wings are usually constructed in three parts: a central hub piece and two separate and diagonal wing pieces (Fig. 4.6).

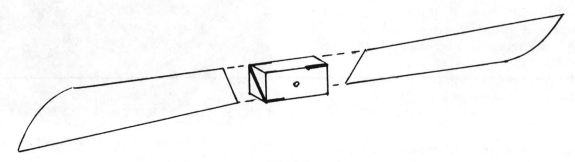

FIG. 4.6

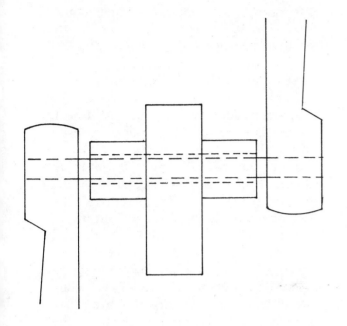

FIG. 4.7

SPLIT-WING MODELS

The Flying Puffin, Nanny the Goat, and Pegasus are examples of the split-wing type of whirligig. In these models, the two blades of the propeller-wing are separated by an axle which passes through the body (Fig. 4.7). The axle can be a brass or steel rod (usually $\frac{1}{8}$" in diameter) or a hardwood dowel ($\frac{1}{4}$" in diameter).

I tend to use a wooden axle on heavier wings, because the wing will adhere to it better over a period of time than it will to a metal rod. Sometimes the wooden hub shrinks and separates from the rod. When wooden axles wear out, they can easily be replaced.

A $\frac{1}{8}$" *metal rod* can be threaded at both ends and, if the hubs are bored with a $\frac{7}{64}$" bit, the wings can easily be turned onto the rod. Adding glue will firmly secure them. Detailed instructions are given for the construction of the Flying Puffin, shown in Fig. 4.8, as an example of how to go about making a split-wing whirligig.

FIG. 4.8

FIG. 4.9

The Flying Puffin

MATERIALS
Body block: $\frac{3}{4}$" × $4\frac{3}{4}$" × $13\frac{1}{2}$"
Wing base (2): $\frac{3}{4}$" × $\frac{3}{4}$" × 2"
Blades (2): $\frac{1}{4}$" × 3" × 7"
Hubs (2): $\frac{3}{4}$" × $\frac{3}{4}$" × $1\frac{1}{2}$"
Pivot socket liner: 2" of $\frac{7}{32}$" brass tubing
Socket cap: one 16d nail end
Spindle: one 16d nail, head cut off
Axle: 4" of $\frac{1}{4}$" hardwood dowel
Sleeve through body: $2\frac{1}{2}$" of $\frac{5}{8}$" tubing

CONSTRUCTION

1. Trace the Flying Puffin design on the wood, marking the positions of the hub (H) and pivot point (P), as well as the outlines of the features. Cut out the figure and drill the socket hole, which may be $\frac{7}{32}$" brass or other metal tubing. Place a cut-off nail end, rounded with a file, in the bottom of the socket as a cap. Smooth and round out the body with sandpaper. Restore the details of the head and beak

for painting. Cut out the wing bases and sand them.

2. Drill a $\frac{5}{16}$" hole through the body at H and through the middle of the wing bases. Glue the wing bases to the body at H, making sure the holes line up. Use the $\frac{5}{16}$" metal tubing for this purpose. Check to see that the $\frac{1}{4}$" dowel will turn easily in the sleeve.

3. Cut out the two wing shapes; trim them down as much as you can and curve the edges. Leave the ends flat where they will attach to the hub piece. Cut out the two hub pieces and drill them with a $\frac{1}{4}$" bit about $\frac{1}{2}$" from the ends. On these pieces, determine where to cut the $\frac{1}{8}$" diagonal slots where the two wings will be attached, remembering the propeller principle. The slots are $\frac{1}{2}$" deep. Glue the wings in the slots, keeping in mind that the long, straight edge of the wing should be parallel to the body. The body and wings are painted separately. Take time to get the details of the Puffin head and beak accurate.

4. Cut out the axle, which ordinarily will be 4" long. Begin with one wing. With glue, drive the axle into the wing hub hole. Insert the axle, with a $\frac{1}{4}$" or $\frac{3}{8}$" washer in place through the body, and attach the other wing, with washer. Brads may be driven through the hubs to secure the axle. Some petroleum jelly or grease may be applied to the axle as it is being inserted.

Other Types

The same construction principles apply to all split-wing whirligigs. The Standing Puffin seen in Fig. 4.9 shows that such wings work on vertical objects as well; that whirligig is constructed in the same way.

Pegasus, shown in Fig. 4.10, is quite similar to the Puffin in construction and, while the wings can be made with hubs and separate vanes, the model illustrated has simpler wings. The body is $\frac{3}{4}$" × 8" × $11\frac{1}{2}$". Two wing bases are needed ($\frac{3}{4}$" × $\frac{3}{4}$" × 2"). The wings, including the hub, can be cut from a single piece of wood ($\frac{3}{4}$" × 2" × $5\frac{1}{2}$"). Drill the $\frac{1}{4}$"

26

FIG. 4.10

hole through the hubs at the points indicated in the illustration. Then shape the wings, remembering that they must turn in opposite directions when attached. Drill a $^3/_8$" hole through the body and the wing bases at H, and glue the bases to the body. Insert the sleeve or liner and test the $^1/_4$" dowel/axle in it. Attach the tail. Paint all parts white and attach the wings.

Nanny the Goat has a unique balancing problem: in this case, large wings are used as ears, placed near the front end of the figure. With the hub (H) so far forward, the pivot point (P) also must be moved forward, as illustrated. There are a few other differences in Nanny's construction. The ears, made of one piece, are turned in different directions like two blades of a propeller, but they are also carved as scoops, somewhat concave in shape. This makes the ears seem more natural and they catch the wind more efficiently. To keep the ears away from the body, ear bases ($^5/_8$" × $^5/_8$" × 1") are glued to the head. Drill a $^3/_{16}$" hole through the head and bases and insert a brass sleeve. Drill $^7/_{64}$" holes in the ear hubs and attach them to a $^1/_8$" threaded metal axle with adhesive, and put washers in place. A much larger goat can be constructed and, if the head is big enough, a hardwood dowel may be used instead of the metal rod.

MODIFIED WING MODELS

Modern Times

The Modern Times variation in Fig. 4.11 shows how a design can be carried to an interesting extreme. It is a winged type in principle, but no one would take it for a bird. It has a simple body of five blocks of wood glued together, in addition to a propeller base. The propellers are formed of two 12" arms, with tilted wooden blades at the ends; the arms may be longer and they may be of different lengths. This elongated propeller provides a stately movement, but requires nice workmanship and precise balancing. When well balanced, it performs beautifully in even a slight breeze. The dimensions of the materials are shown in the patterns.

1. Make five wood blocks as indicated; glue and nail them together in an overlapping fashion. As with other whirligigs, estab-

FIG. 4.11

27

lish a centerline and mark a place for the hub (H) and the pivot point (P). At P, drill a $7/32$" hole and line the socket with brass tubing. Cap this with a 16d nail end or a small roundheaded screw. Drill small pilot holes in the propeller blocks and glue them at H.

2. Cut out two propeller arms of the same length (12"), or of different lengths (12" and 14", for example). Make four propeller blades; they may be of different shapes. Cut the end of each arm at an angle to hold the blades at opposite angles, like propellers. Make sure the two arms will turn in different directions from each other. Glue the blades to the arms.

3. Find the balance point of the arms and mark them. Drill through the points with a $3/16$" bit and line the hub with brass tubing.

4. Paint the parts before assembly. The body may be a solid color, but the blades look good when they are of varied colors. Attach the arms to the propeller block with $1\frac{1}{4}$" No. 6 brass round-headed screws and washers. Mount the whirligig on a 16d nail with head removed.

SUMMARY OF MATERIAL SIZES FOR WINGED WHIRLIGIGS
(in inches)

WOOD

Project	Body Block	Wing Base	Wings
American Goldfinch	$3/4 \times 1\frac{1}{2} \times 5\frac{1}{4}$	$1/2 \times 1/2 \times 3/4$	$5/8 \times 5/8 \times 5\frac{1}{2}$
Eastern Bluebird	$3/4 \times 1\frac{1}{2} \times 6\frac{1}{2}$	$1/2 \times 1/2 \times 1$	$3/4 \times 3/4 \times 6$
Cardinal	$3/4 \times 3/4 \times 8\frac{1}{2}$	$5/8 \times 5/8 \times 1\frac{1}{4}$	$3/4 \times 1 \times 8$
Robin	$3/4 \times 3\frac{1}{2} \times 10$	$3/4 \times 3/4 \times 1\frac{1}{2}$	$3/4 \times 1 \times 8$
Flying Puffin	$3/4 \times 4\frac{3}{4} \times 13\frac{1}{2}$	$3/4 \times 3/4 \times 1\frac{1}{2}$	$1/4 \times 4 \times 7$
Standing Puffin	$3/4 \times 4\frac{1}{2} \times 10$	$3/4 \times 3/4 \times 1\frac{1}{2}$	$1/4 \times 3\frac{1}{2} \times 6$
Pegasus	$3/4 \times 8 \times 11\frac{1}{2}$	$3/4 \times 3/4 \times 2$	$3/4 \times 2 \times 5\frac{1}{2}$
Nanny the Goat	$3/4 \times 8 \times 10$	$5/8 \times 5/8 \times 1$	$3/4 \times 2\frac{1}{4} \times 5$
Modern Times	See drawing	See drawing	See drawing

OTHER MATERIALS

Project	Wing Sleeves	Axle	Socket Liners	Spindles
American Goldfinch	$3/16$ tubing	$1\frac{1}{4}$ No. 6 screws	$7/32$ tubing	16d nail
Eastern Bluebird	$3/16$ tubing	$1\frac{1}{4}$ No. 6 screws	$7/32$ tubing	16d nail
Cardinal	$3/16$ tubing	$1\frac{1}{4}$ No. 6 screws	$7/32$ tubing	16d nail
Robin	$3/16$ tubing	$1\frac{1}{4}$ No. 6 screws	$7/32$ tubing	16d nail
Flying Puffin	$5/16$ tubing	$1/4$ dowel	$7/32$ tubing	16d nail
Standing Puffin	$5/16$ tubing	$1/4$ dowel	$7/32$ tubing	16d nail
Pegasus	$5/16$ tubing	$1/4$ dowel	$7/32$ tubing	16d nail
Nanny the Goat	$1/8$ tubing (head)	$3/32$ brass rod	$7/32$ tubing	16d nail
Modern Times	$3/16$ tubing	$1\frac{1}{4}$ No. 6 screws	$7/32$ tubing	16d nail

FIG. 4.12

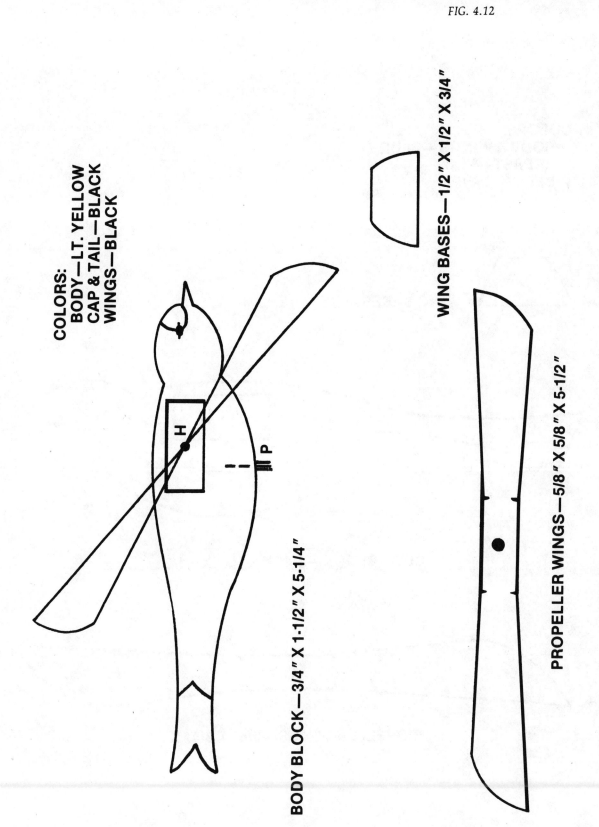

COLORS:
BODY—LT. YELLOW
CAP & TAIL—BLACK
WINGS—BLACK

WING BASES—1/2" X 1/2" X 3/4"

BODY BLOCK—3/4" X 1-1/2" X 5-1/4"

PROPELLER WINGS—5/8" X 5/8" X 5-1/2"

COLORS:
    BODY & WINGS—BLUE
    BREAST—PINK
    BELLY—WHITE

WING BASES—1/2″ X 1/2″ X 1″

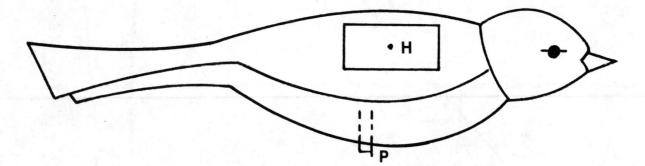

BODY BLOCK—3/4″ X 1-1/2″ X 6-1/2″

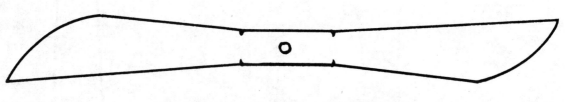

PROPELLER WINGS—3/4″ X 3/4″ X 6″

Cardinal

FIG. 4.14

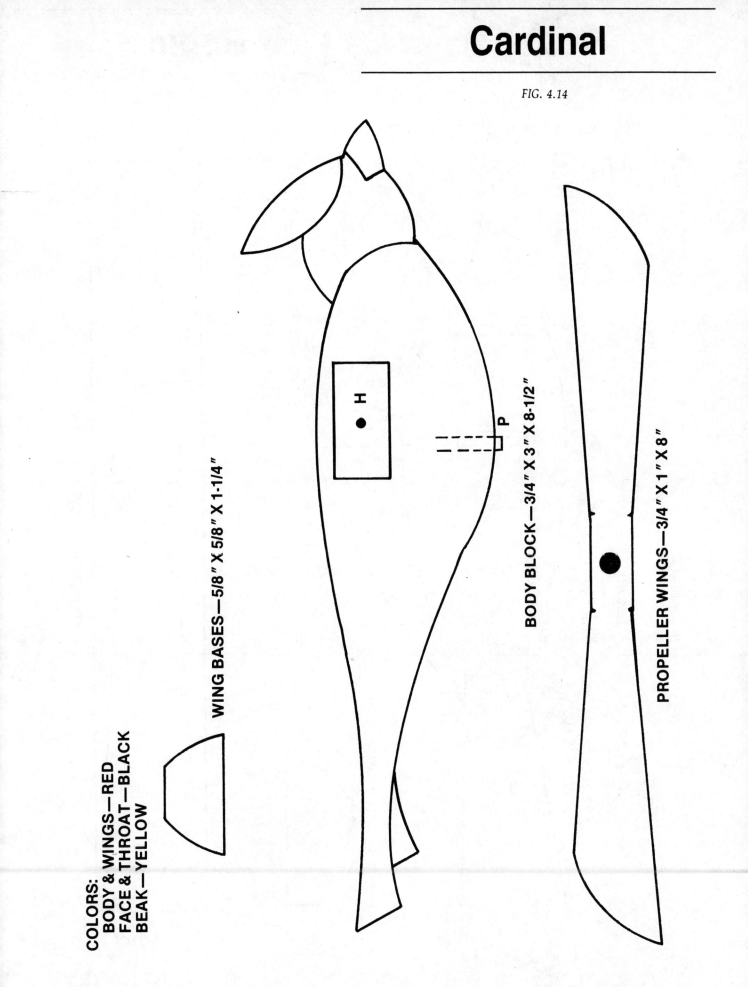

COLORS:
BODY & WINGS—RED
FACE & THROAT—BLACK
BEAK—YELLOW

WING BASES—5/8 " X 5/8 " X 1-1/4 "

BODY BLOCK—3/4 " X 3 " X 8-1/2 "

PROPELLER WINGS—3/4 " X 1 " X 8 "

31

Robin

FIG. 4.15

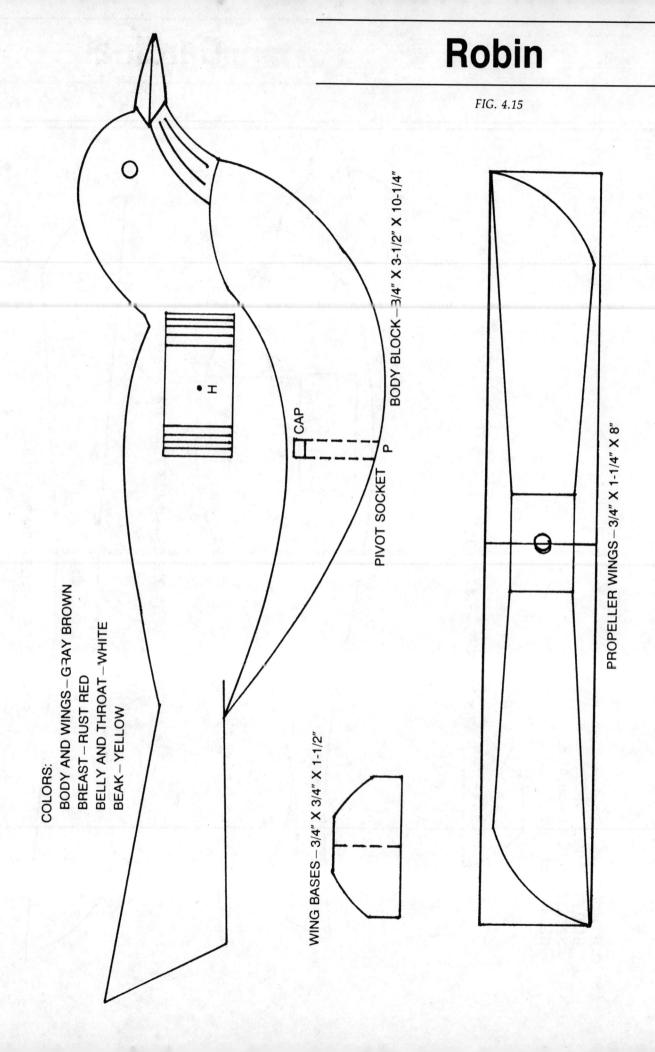

COLORS:
BODY AND WINGS—GRAY BROWN
BREAST—RUST RED
BELLY AND THROAT—WHITE
BEAK—YELLOW

BODY BLOCK—3/4" X 3-1/2" X 10-1/4"

PIVOT SOCKET

CAP

PROPELLER WINGS—3/4" X 1-1/4" X 8"

WING BASES—3/4" X 3/4" X 1-1/2"

Danny the Dragon

FIG. 4.16

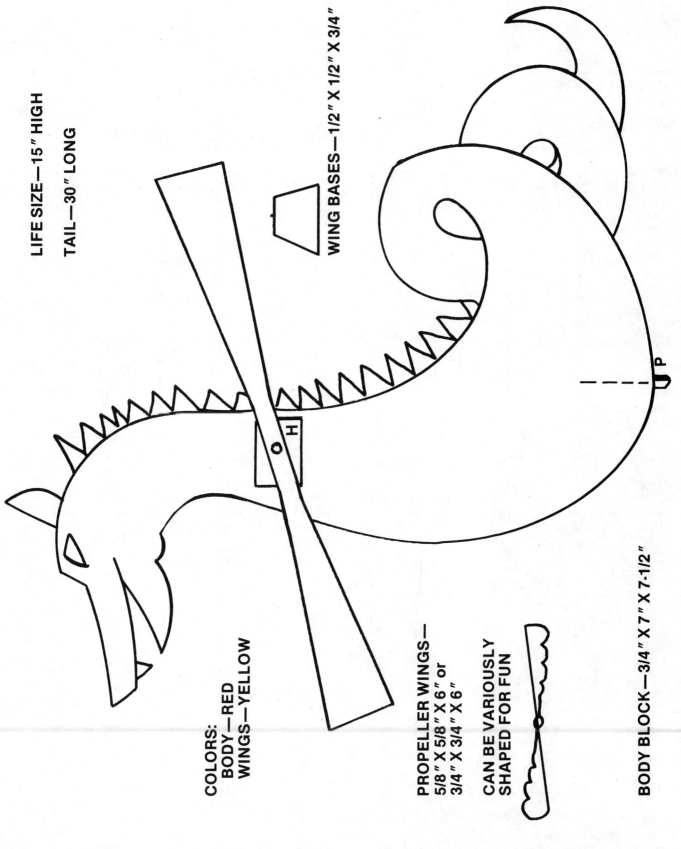

LIFE SIZE—15″ HIGH

TAIL—30″ LONG

WING BASES—1/2″ X 1/2″ X 3/4″

COLORS:
BODY—RED
WINGS—YELLOW

PROPELLER WINGS—
5/8″ X 5/8″ X 6″ or
3/4″ X 3/4″ X 6″

CAN BE VARIOUSLY
SHAPED FOR FUN

BODY BLOCK—3/4″ X 7″ X 7-1/2″

Flying Puffin

FIG. 4.17

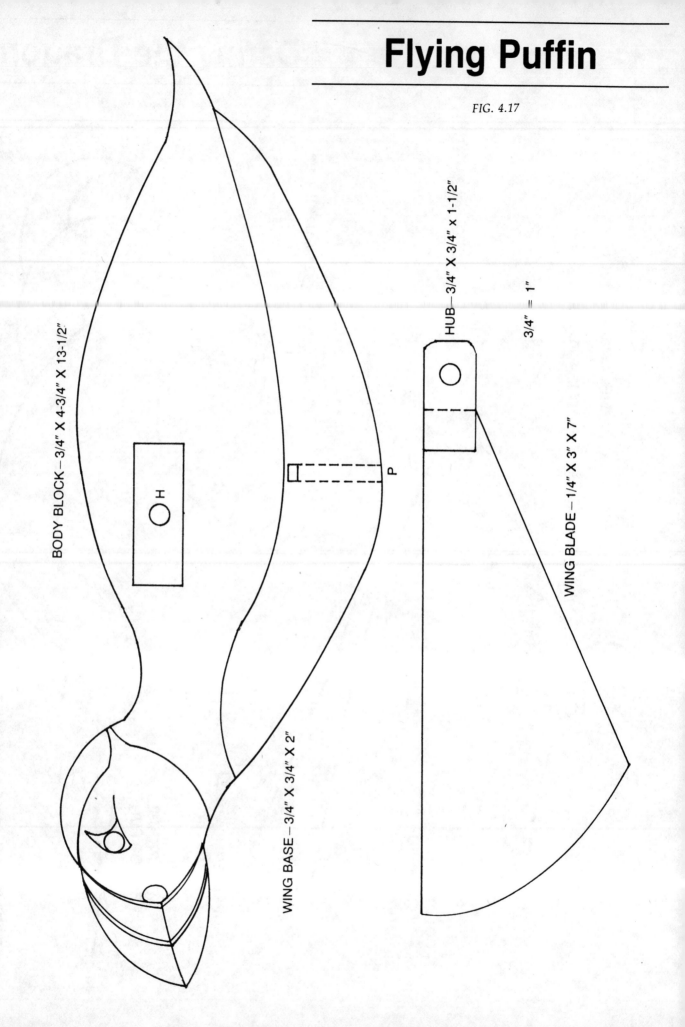

BODY BLOCK—3/4" X 4-3/4" X 13-1/2"

H

WING BASE—3/4" X 3/4" X 2"

P

HUB—3/4" X 3/4" x 1-1/2"

3/4" = 1"

WING BLADE—1/4" X 3" X 7"

Standing Puffin

FIG. 4.18

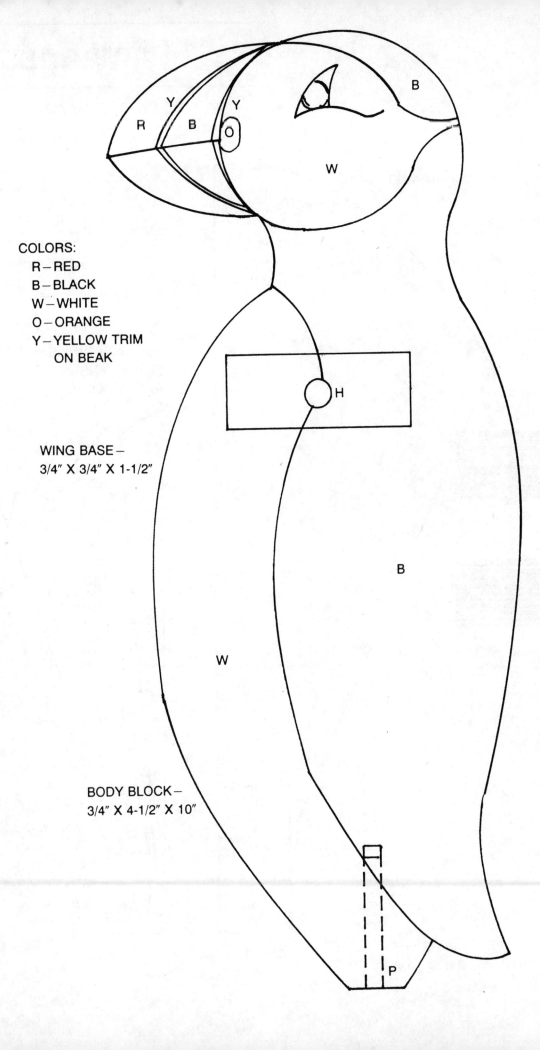

COLORS:
R – RED
B – BLACK
W – WHITE
O – ORANGE
Y – YELLOW TRIM
   ON BEAK

WING BASE –
3/4" X 3/4" X 1-1/2"

BODY BLOCK –
3/4" X 4-1/2" X 10"

Wings

FIG. 4.19

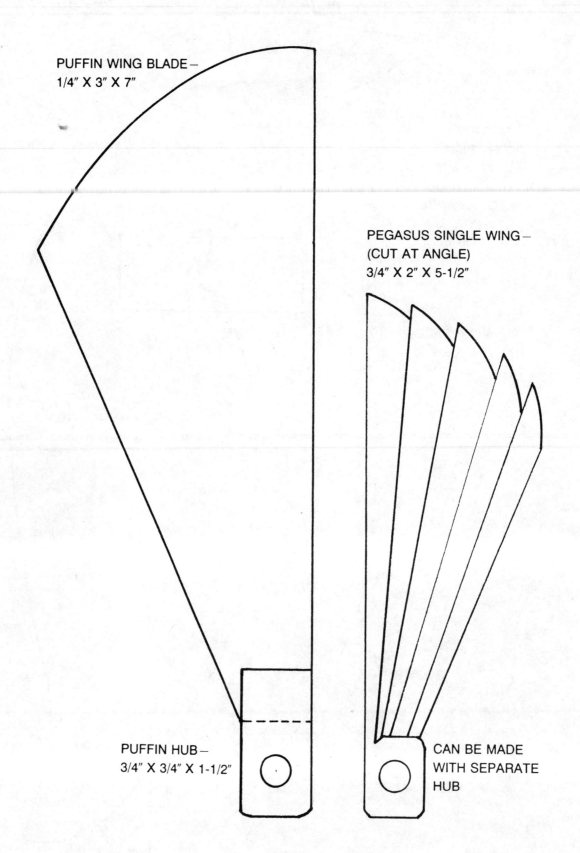

PUFFIN WING BLADE—
1/4" X 3" X 7"

PEGASUS SINGLE WING—
(CUT AT ANGLE)
3/4" X 2" X 5-1/2"

PUFFIN HUB—
3/4" X 3/4" X 1-1/2"

CAN BE MADE
WITH SEPARATE
HUB

Pegasus

FIG. 4.20

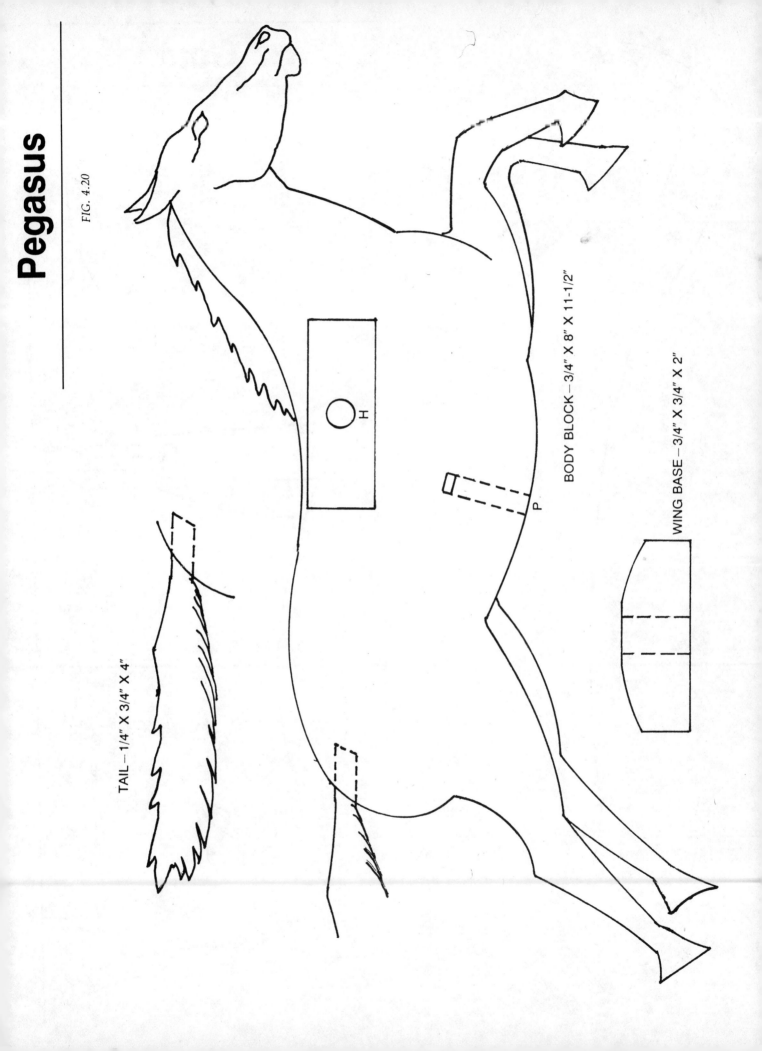

TAIL — 1/4" X 3/4" X 4"

BODY BLOCK — 3/4" X 8" X 11-1/2"

WING BASE — 3/4" X 3/4" X 2"

Goat

FIG. 4.21

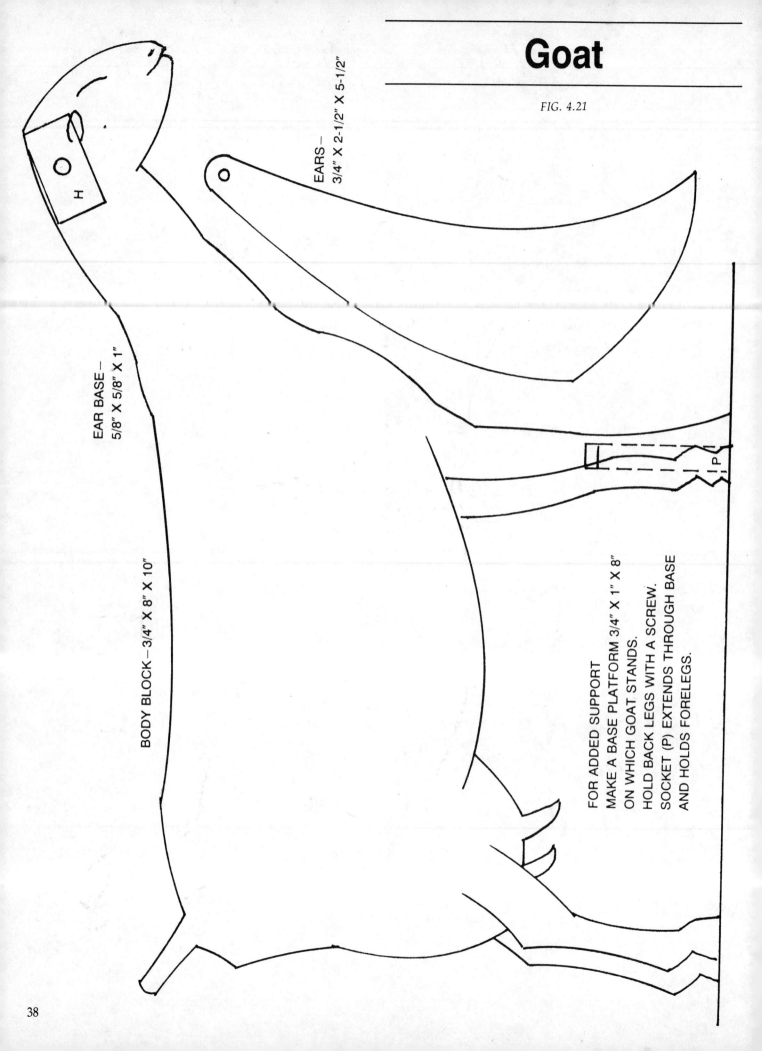

EARS—
3/4" X 2-1/2" X 5-1/2"

EAR BASE—
5/8" X 5/8" X 1"

BODY BLOCK—3/4" X 8" X 10"

FOR ADDED SUPPORT
MAKE A BASE PLATFORM 3/4" X 1" X 8"
ON WHICH GOAT STANDS.
HOLD BACK LEGS WITH A SCREW.
SOCKET (P) EXTENDS THROUGH BASE
AND HOLDS FORELEGS.

FIG. 4.22

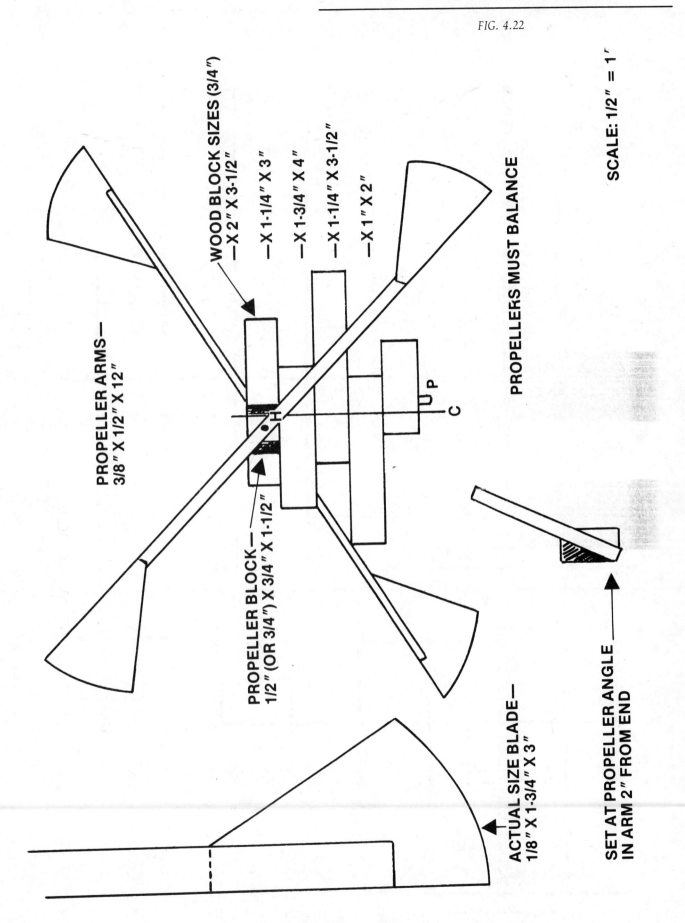

WOOD BLOCK SIZES (3/4")
—X 2" X 3-1/2"
—X 1-1/4" X 3"
—X 1-3/4" X 4"
—X 1-1/4" X 3-1/2"
—X 1" X 2"

PROPELLERS MUST BALANCE

SCALE: 1/2" = 1'

PROPELLER ARMS—
3/8" X 1/2" X 12"

PROPELLER BLOCK—
1/2" (OR 3/4") X 3/4" X 1-1/2"

ACTUAL SIZE BLADE—
1/8" X 1-3/4" X 3"

SET AT PROPELLER ANGLE —
IN ARM 2" FROM END

Modern Times

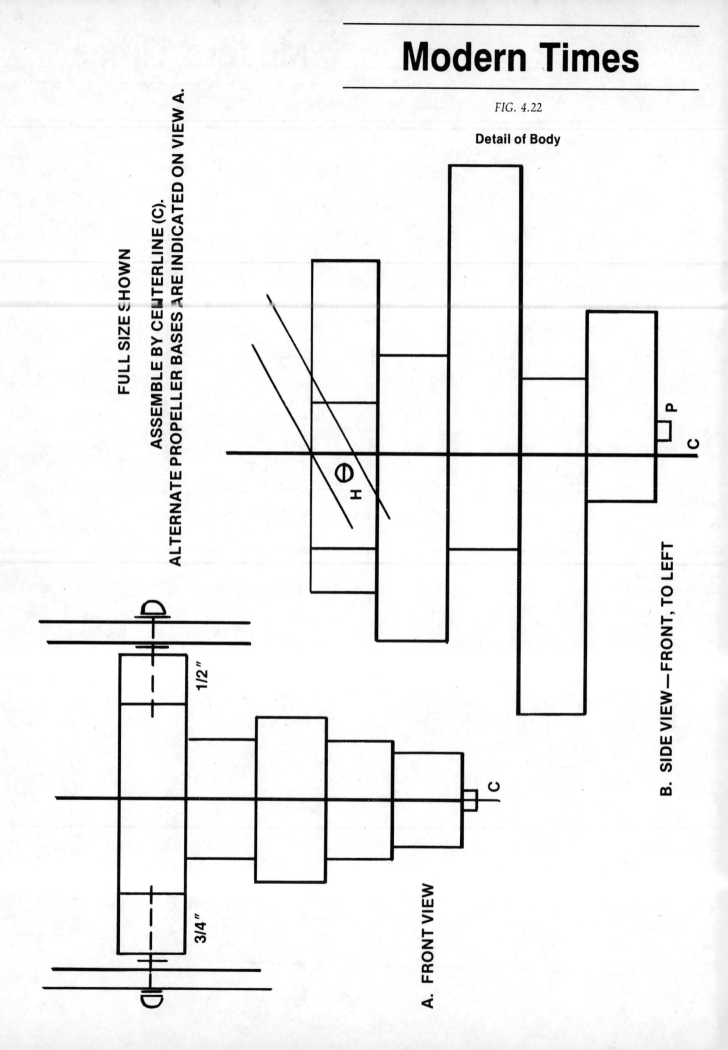

FIG. 4.22

Detail of Body

FULL SIZE SHOWN

ASSEMBLE BY CENTERLINE (C).

ALTERNATE PROPELLER BASES ARE INDICATED ON VIEW A.

1/2"

3/4"

B. SIDE VIEW—FRONT, TO LEFT

A. FRONT VIEW

5

Construction of Arm-Waving Whirligigs

Classic arm-waving whirligigs are designed to operate entirely by balance, and the proper relationship between the pivot and the hub is all-important, as in the relative positions of the hub (H) to the pivot (P) to the centerline (C) in Fig. 5.1. In some models this will place the shoulders in an unnatural position, but in whirligigs a bit of oddity is permissible, even expected. The arm-waving whirligig works best when H is somewhat forward of P.

To test this, I constructed a test board measuring $\frac{3}{4}'' \times 2'' \times 8''$ with a set of arms attached 2" from the top and on the centerline, and three pivot-point sockets (Fig. 5.2). Pivot P-1 was $\frac{1}{4}''$ forward of the center, pivot P-2 was at the center, and pivot P-3 was $\frac{1}{4}''$ back of the center. When tested on Pivot P-1, the board faced the wind and stalled and acted like a weathervane. The arms flapped once and stopped. On pivot P-2, the whirligig was erratic and started and stopped and started again, only to stop finally. On pivot P-3, the action was correct, and the whirligig twisted and turned in the wind.

The balance point of an upright figure is not easy to determine, and an arbitrary decision must be made as to its location. It is easiest to assume that the balance point more or less corresponds to the centerline running vertically

FIG. 5.1

41

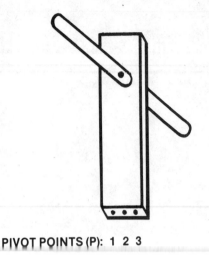

PIVOT POINTS (P): 1 2 3

FIG. 5.2

up the figure. The figure may be stood up on its feet or base and the centerline drawn with a square. The pivot socket is placed slightly to the rear of that line and the hub socket located slightly in front of it. In the working models at the end of this section, these points are $\frac{5}{8}$" apart (Uncle Sam) and $\frac{1}{4}$" apart (Gentleman Jim).

In new designs, these locations must be tested, and I usually try two test pivot sockets on new whirligigs. Old designs should be tested also. I have found that antique whirligigs, such as those seen in museums, or in books, do not necessarily operate properly when copied. In some cases, this may be because the figures are incomplete or have been altered. In others, the whirligigs may not have been intended as working models. Testing primarily means moving the pivot forward or back until the wind toy works properly.

BASIC STEPS

Design

Select a design and draw a front and side view of the person or object. There is no limit to the subjects or figures you can make into arm-waving whirligigs; it is entirely up to your imagination. Anyone can copy a figure or make a crude drawing of it and that is all one needs for a start. It will become easier as you

go along; when you come to the actual carving, the figure will take on a life of its own. In drawing the figure, I usually use graph paper with 4 or 8 squares to the inch. A simple human figure whirligig will stand about 9" or 10" tall, so I mark that off first on the graph paper. In making an original model, draw the front of the figure on the left side of the paper and the side view or profile on the right. In the middle draw the arm or paw or whatever. This permits all parts to correspond with each other.

There are two particular points to put on the figure: the location of the hub (H) and the socket or pivot hole (P). Place H where the shoulder axle will be and P at the bottom in the center of the block, but behind a perpendicular line drawn through H. See the various illustrations of whirligigs in this section for guidance. Draw the arms next, allowing for the extension of the arms from the body and for any attachments. The completed drawing should include all particulars that will guide in carving and painting, such as the details of the features, clothing, colors, and so on.

Patterns

Make patterns of both side and front views, and the arms. When the drawing is finished, trace it on thin cardboard and cut out the pattern with scissors. A pattern is easier to apply to a wood block than tracing directly on the block itself; also the pattern can be used again. First, draw centerlines on all sides of the block and on the top and bottom. Then place the patterns on the block and outline the figure. Pay particular attention to the location of the hub hole (H) on both sides of the block. The socket hole (P) is usually located behind the centerline traversing the block. Stand the block upright and, with the aid of a square, draw a line through the hub and continue it along the bottom of the block. The point P should be located about $\frac{1}{4}$" behind that line.

Hub and Pivot Point

Drill the hub hole (H) and the socket (P). To make sure the hub is horizontal, particularly in a large figure and if a precision drill press is not available, drill from each side about halfway through. The hole must be large enough to accommodate the metal tube that will be used as a sleeve. After drilling, make sure the tube will fit without binding or bending. Do not leave it in the hole while carving. Drill point P about 2" deep with a $\frac{7}{32}$" bit. Place a $\frac{7}{32}$" piece of brass tubing in the hole as a socket liner. Then drive a 16d nail point into the base or place a small roundheaded screw there. It will serve as a cap, to prevent the spindle from wearing through the wood.

Cutting and Carving

With a coping saw, compass saw or band saw, cut out the pattern on the block. Sometimes only the profile view is necessary and the carving can proceed from there. But if the front must be cut out as well, here is where the cardboard patterns are helpful. They will show where the cuts must be made after the surface has been removed from the previous cutting. In some cases, no sawing is necessary, and all cutting can be done with carving knives. Then carve the figure. Every woodcarver has a variety of knives and a favorite knife. A beginner should probably have a good basic knife, of a sloyd variety, and a small carving set using replaceable blades. Remember the basic rules: cut away from yourself as much as possible, and allow for knife slips. It is fun to carve and see the block come to life.

Arms and Attachments

Make the arms. Draw the pattern on each arm block. Then drill the hub with a hole the diameter of the axle or somewhat smaller. Saw out the arm outline. Mark the ends for diagonal cutting. Put the arms against the figure and check to make sure that when the wind blows the arms will act as a single propeller, though divided by an axle. While the arm at the top of the shoulder may be rounded, as may the back of the arm, most of the arm must be made quite flat, thinned down to about $\frac{1}{8}$". Both arms must be evenly balanced. Place them on a temporary axle; if they are out of

balance the heavier arm should be trimmed down. The attachments (flags, towels, baskets, etc.) are made of thin pieces of wood, $\frac{1}{16}$" to $\frac{1}{8}$" thick. Glue them to the arms so that they project away from the body.

Final Assembly

Paint the parts before final assembly. The arm hubs can be touched up after the arms are attached. The hub sleeve should be in place. Press the axle into one arm hub with a bit of glue. Put a washer on the axle before passing it through the body. Similarly press or hammer the rod carefully into the other arm with washer attached.

If you are using a $\frac{1}{8}$" metal rod, drill a $\frac{7}{64}$" hole in the arms. Thread the rod at both ends and turn the arms, with glue, onto the rod. Mount the model on a post or pole with a 16d nail, with head cut off and rounded, as a spindle, and watch it turn and twist in the wind.

Each of the models described below has different construction characteristics. Four are standard whirligigs: Uncle Sam, Gentleman Jim, Signaling Sailor, and Flower Lady. Another four—Colonial Dame, Soldier, Santa Claus, and Doggie—are supplemented with a rudder assembly. Man Rowing Boat and Indian in Canoe are examples of modified forms.

STANDARD MODELS

The standard arm-waving whirligig is an independent figure which stands by itself, waving its arms and holding some item or implement relating to its identity. There are two types of standard figures: the flat or profile figure, and the figure sculpted in the round. Among the working drawings at the end of this section, Uncle Sam (Fig. 5.3) is a flat whirligig and the Signaling Sailor is a figure fully carved in the round. Historically, Uncle Sam came into being in the middle of the 19th century and was formalized by the cartoonist Thomas Nast in the 1890s. The Signaling Sailor is of a type that has been around since the early 1800s. Because they are slightly differ-

FIG. 5.3

FIG. 5.4

ent, the following notes will separately detail their construction.

Uncle Sam

MATERIALS
Body block: $\frac{3}{4}'' \times 1\frac{3}{4}'' \times 9''$
Arms (2): $\frac{3}{4}'' \times 1\frac{3}{4}'' \times 4\frac{1}{2}''$
Flags (2): $\frac{1}{8}'' \times 1\frac{1}{4}'' \times 1\frac{3}{4}''$
Axle: $\frac{1}{8}''$ brass or steel rod, about $2\frac{1}{2}''$ long
Sleeve (H): $\frac{3}{16}''$ brass tubing
Socket liner (P): $\frac{7}{32}''$ tubing, about $1\frac{1}{2}''$ long
Socket cap: 12d nail end, or small screw

CONSTRUCTION
1. Trace the figure outline on wood and cut it out. Drill a $\frac{7}{32}''$ hole at P for the pivot socket. Put the liner in place and cap the socket. Then drill a hole for the axle at point H, and insert a sleeve. (*Note:* to make sure the arms will stand away from the body, shoulders may be added to the top of the figure. These are made of pieces $\frac{1}{2}'' \times \frac{3}{4}'' \times 1''$. The hub hole (H) will then be drilled through shoulders and figure.) The head may be slightly carved to suggest the principal features.
2. Cut out arms and plan their position and the angles at which they will be cut. Drill a $\frac{1}{8}''$ hole or smaller near the top of the arms at H. Then cut them diagonally to form the propeller, keeping lower part flat and thinned to $\frac{1}{8}''$. Balance the arms.
3. Cut out the flags and glue them to the arms, making sure the flags will angle out from the body. Paint all parts before attaching the arms with a $\frac{1}{8}''$ rod, threaded at the ends, as an axle through the sleeves at H.

Signaling Sailor

Most arm-waving whirligigs are carved in the round, as is the sailor in Fig. 5.4; the steps below supplement the instruction provided previously.

MATERIALS
Body block: $1\frac{3}{4}'' \times 2\frac{1}{4}'' \times 9\frac{1}{4}''$
Arms (2): $\frac{3}{4}'' \times 1'' \times 5''$

Flags (2): $\frac{1}{8}$" × $1\frac{1}{2}$" × $1\frac{3}{4}$"
Axle: $\frac{1}{8}$" brass or steel rod, 3" long
Sleeve (H): $\frac{3}{16}$" brass tubing
Socket liner (P): $\frac{7}{32}$" tubing, $1\frac{1}{2}$" long
Socket cap: 16d nail end

CONSTRUCTION

1. Trace the pattern on the front and side of the wood block. (Sometimes it is advisable to trace the corresponding pattern on the back and opposite side, as well). First drill a $\frac{7}{32}$" hole at P for the socket and a $\frac{3}{16}$" hole through the block at H for the axle. Then cut out the pattern with a band saw or other saws. Put the socket liner in place with a cap. You can then stand it on a mounting as you work with it.

2. Carve the figure out carefully and sand it. Then cut out the arms and flags. Drill the arms with a $\frac{1}{8}$" hole (or slightly smaller if rod is threaded at ends) where the hub will be. Holding the arms against the body, mark their ends for the proper propeller shape. Carve them out; the bottom half should be quite flat. Glue the flags to the arms, making sure they will be away from the body. Paint the parts separately before attaching the arms with glue to the $\frac{1}{8}$" rod, washers in place between the arms and body.

Gentleman Jim

Gentleman Jim is made from a block of wood $1\frac{1}{2}$" × $1\frac{1}{2}$" × 9". He can be carved as illustrated, or designers can add their own features. He has been bald and appeared with a derby hat. He has sometimes been white and sometimes black. He has been straight-legged and bow-legged. He can be almost anything, but traditionally he looks like a prosperous planter/horseman from another era. The base pivot and the arm hub are placed in the same relative positions as those for Uncle Sam.

With Gentleman Jim, the actual construction of the pivot requires special attention. In figures with carved, separated legs, as in this one, it is usually necessary to provide two additional items.

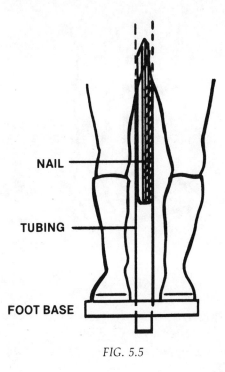

NAIL

TUBING

FOOT BASE

FIG. 5.5

First, a foot base is needed. This can be made of standard $\frac{1}{4}$" lath stripping, trimmed just wide enough for the figure to stand on. This base holds the pivot socket in position (Fig. 5.5).

Second, the pivot tubing must be extended up past the inside of the legs and into the body. The base is drilled for the socket tubing. When the tubing is in place, the socket itself can be shortened by cutting a nail to the correct length and driving it up through the tubing into the body. The socket can thus be made to any desirable length. The major problem is making certain the tubing is set in a vertical position.

Some antique whirligigs have a different type of pivot structure, consisting of two metal plates, one at the base and the other up between the legs about knee level. The lower plate has a larger hole, and the upper one has a smaller aperture. The whirligig rests on a sharp, tapered spindle, wider at the bottom than the top, as shown in Fig. 5.6.

In some modern weathervanes, the spindle has a ridge on it, and the vane rides on this ridge. Whirligig makers should experiment with pivot structures, and at times need to invent new ones to fit particular designs.

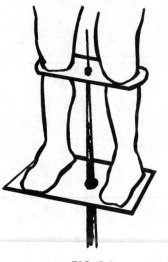

FIG. 5.6

For this figure and others with slender arms, a smaller axle ($\frac{3}{32}$" metal rod) and a smaller sleeve ($\frac{1}{8}$" brass tubing) can be used at the hub.

Flower Lady

It occurred to me one summer that most whirligigs seemed to be of men. I noticed a woman in a garden gathering flowers and I thought of a flower lady who waves baskets of flowers over her head. I wasn't sure it would work as a whirligig, but it did; the Flower Lady shown in Fig. 5.7 is now a popular model!

The Flower Lady is 9 inches tall and is carved from a block $1\frac{3}{4}$" $\times$ $2\frac{1}{4}$" $\times$ 9". The figure should be shapely (Fig. 5.8). The arms are cut from blocks $\frac{3}{4}$" $\times$ 1 x 5", and the baskets are $\frac{1}{8}$" $\times$ $1\frac{3}{4}$" $\times$ 2" and shaped like baskets loaded with flowers. When the arms have been carved and balanced, the flower baskets should be attached; make sure they will extend outward from the body when the arms are in place. Care should be taken in painting this whirligig because much of its attraction comes from the gaily painted flowers and the colors of the woman's dress.

RUDDER ASSEMBLY MODELS

There is an advantage to having some upright whirligigs be ultrasensitive to the wind.

This can be achieved by fitting them with a tail or rudder assembly (Fig. 5.9). The tail may be decorative as well as functional and, as it is usually not a very large affair, it will not detract from the moving figure.

After the figure has been carved and sanded, the tail plane can be attached with water-resistant glue and wire brads. The assembly's base can be made from any 10" to 12" piece of lath stripping which comes in $\frac{1}{4}$" $\times$ $1\frac{1}{4}$" sections. The rudder can be made of the same material, but it should be planed or shaved down to $\frac{1}{16}$" or $\frac{1}{8}$" thickness. It is glued into a slot cut into the assembly base. The tail assembly is then attached at right angles to the figure, projecting from an arm-propeller side.

Soldier, Colonial Dame, Santa and Doggie Models

Although the drawing of the Soldier shows the legs separated, as are many antique whirli-

FIG. 5.7

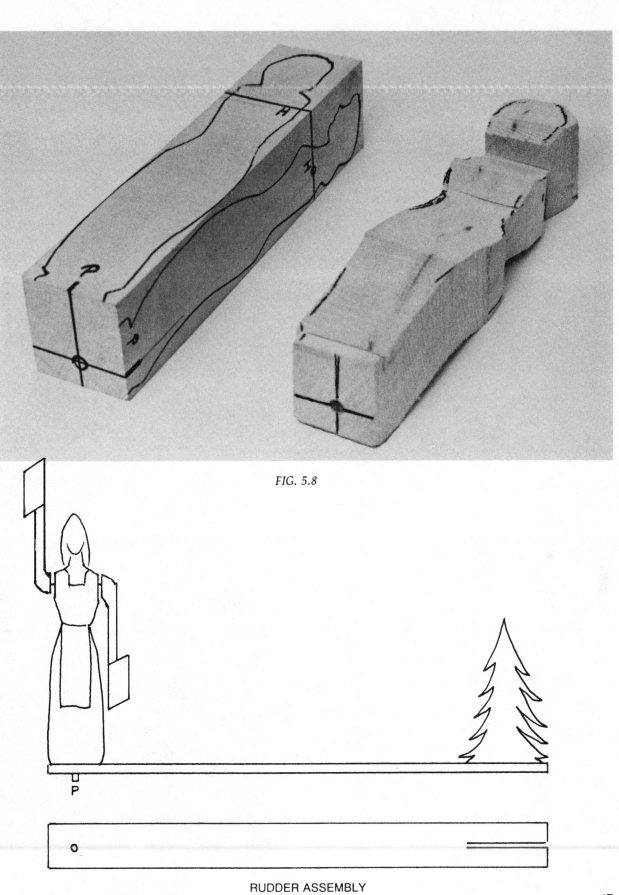

FIG. 5.8

RUDDER ASSEMBLY

FIG. 5.9

FIG. 5.10

gigs, there is no reason why the legs cannot be together and the bottom part solid. This simplifies the placing of the socket in the body. Also, the Colonial Dame's feet need not be carved out and her dress can reach to the base (Fig. 5.10). Santa's legs are not separated and the socket goes directly into the base. In all models, the pivot sockets are drilled with a $\frac{7}{32}$" bit and lined with tubing. The tubing for tail assembly whirligigs should extend about $\frac{1}{2}$" below the base of the figure to permit it to extend through the tail plane, as shown in the illustrations.

The Soldier (Fig. 5.11) is constructed like other models, except for the tail assembly (Fig. 5.12). This consists of a tail extension made of a piece of wood $\frac{1}{4}$" × $1\frac{1}{4}$" × 12". A $\frac{7}{32}$" hole is drilled at one end to permit the socket liner to penetrate. A 2" slot $\frac{1}{8}$" wide is cut into the other end of the tail plane for the rudder. The rudder in this case is a milestone, $\frac{1}{8}$" × $1\frac{1}{2}$" × 3"; it can be of any design and of larger size.

Remember that the tail will cause the whirligig to face sideways into the wind, and that air

FIG. 5.11

48

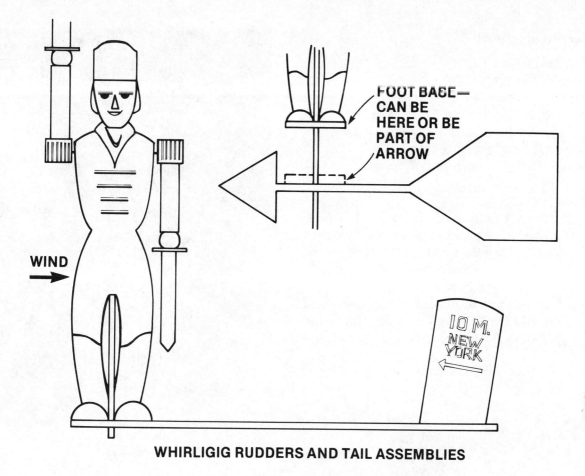

WHIRLIGIG RUDDERS AND TAIL ASSEMBLIES

FIG. 5.12

flow will cause the arms to move in a certain direction. Once I forgot this simple principle and the soldier waved his swords backward instead of forward. The entire tail assembly had to be reversed. So the arms must be cut with the position of the tail in mind, or if the arms are cut first, the tail assembly must be attached on the correct side of the figure.

Colonial Dame is made in the same way, and the suggested rudder is a jug. For Santa Claus it is a Christmas Tree. This whirligig is very popular in the winter holiday season; he happily waves boxes of presents. He can be made smaller or larger; the one for which plans are provided is 9" tall. Because of Santa's girth, larger models require thick wood, or several layers of wood glued together. Also because of his girth, the arms must be double checked to see that they clear the body. While a solid block is preferred, two or more pieces

of wood can be spliced together to make a block. In such a case, the figures should be carved with the front of the figures facing the edges, not the sides, of the wood.

Doggie, the canine whirligig shown in Fig. 5.13, has been added to this section to show that the arm-waving type is not limited to human figures. Doggie's paws wave cheerfully in the wind, and his favorite fire hydrant is nearby. Appropriately, he has a tail assembly.

MODIFIED PROPELLER MODELS

There are a few whirligigs which, because of their size and shape, are modified arm-wavers. Among these are Man Rowing Boat and Indian in Canoe. Both of these are old whirligig favorites.

49

Man Rowing Boat

MATERIALS

Boat: $3\frac{3}{4}'' \times 5\frac{1}{4}'' \times 24''$
Man: $\frac{3}{4}'' \times 4'' \times 4''$
Shoulders: $\frac{3}{4}'' \times \frac{3}{4}'' \times 3''$
Axle: $\frac{1}{4}''$ hardwood dowel, about 3" long
Sleeve (H): $\frac{5}{16}''$ metal tubing
Socket (P): $\frac{3}{8}''$ tension pin, 2" long

CONSTRUCTION

1. Trace the pattern of the boat onto wood, marking the position of the pivot hole (P) and locating the hub (H) line. Drill for the 2" tension pin and inset it with a cap. File and sand the boat body.

2. Cut out the head and shoulders. Hold the head to the boat and determine the position of H by sight, or by running a

FIG. 5.14a

perpendicular line up the body with a square. Hold a shoulder to the head to see if the H point doesn't put the shoulders too high. It will be about 1" above the top of the boat. Drill a $\frac{5}{16}''$ hole through the figure at H, and also through the top of the shoulders, about $\frac{1}{2}''$ from the end. Glue these parts together, fitting a $\frac{5}{16}''$ piece of tubing through the holes. When dry, fit the shoulders over the boat so H is in proper relationship to P. Do not force the shoulders on; if the overhang is tight, file or cut them down. Then glue and nail the assembly in position. Brads or small nails can be driven through the shoulders from the sides, and through the body from the top.

3. Cut out the arm/oar pieces. Drill $\frac{1}{4}''$ holes, $\frac{1}{2}''$ from the ends, for the axle. Holding the arms to the shoulders, mark the proper angle for each end to be cut, so that it will act as the blade of a propeller. With carving tools, cut the tops of

FIG. 5.13

50

FIG. 5.14b

FIG. 5.15

the arms to shape, so they represent arms. The bottom part (about 4") should be made as flat as possible, to resemble oars. Paint all the parts when this is done.

4. Attach the arms to the ¼" dowel-axle with glue, using ¼" washers between the arms and the shoulders. A touch of petroleum jelly or grease may be placed on the axle to ease movement.

Indian in Canoe

The Indian in Canoe, shown in Fig. 5.15, is constructed in somewhat the same way, with a few differences. The hub point (H) is placed slightly behind the pivot point (P). The Indian leans forward and the shoulders (¾" × ¾" × 2¾") are placed upright, or also leaning slightly forward.

The canoe is ¾" × 4" × 24", and the head/body is ¾" × 4" × 4". An eagle feather can be glued into a hole in the head. The arms/paddles measure ¾" × 1" × 9" and, as with the oars, the top part is rounded to resemble arms, and the bottom part, about 4", is shaped like a paddle.

SUMMARY OF MATERIAL SIZES FOR ARM-WAVING WHIRLIGIGS
(in inches)

WOOD

Project	Body Block	Arms
Uncle Sam	¾ × 1½ × 9	¾ × 1¼ × 4½
Gentleman Jim	1½ × 1¾ × 9	¾ × 1 × 5½
Signaling Sailor	1¾ × 2¼ × 9¼	¾ × 1 × 5
Flower Lady	1¾ × 2¼ × 9	1 × 1 × 5
Colonial Dame	2 × 2¾ × 8¼	¾ × ⅞ × 5
Soldier	1½ × 1½ × 9½	¾ × 1 × 5½
Santa Claus	2¼ × 2½ × 9	¾ × 1 × 5½
Doggie	¾ × 4½ × 8¼	¾ × ¾ × 4½
Man Rowing	¾ × 5½ × 24	¾ × 1 × 9
Indian in Canoe	¾ × 4 × 24	¾ × 1 × 9

OTHER MATERIALS

Project	Arm Sleeves	Arm Axle	Socket Liners	Spindle
All types, except two itemized below	⅛ or 3/16 brass tubing	3/32 brass rod or ⅛ brass or steel rod	7/32 brass tubing	16d nail
Man in Boat	5/16 tubing in body	¼ wood dowel	⅜ tension pin	20d–30d nail
Indian in Canoe	5/16 tubing in body	¼ wood dowel	⅜ tension pin	20d–30d nail

Uncle Sam

FIG. 5.16

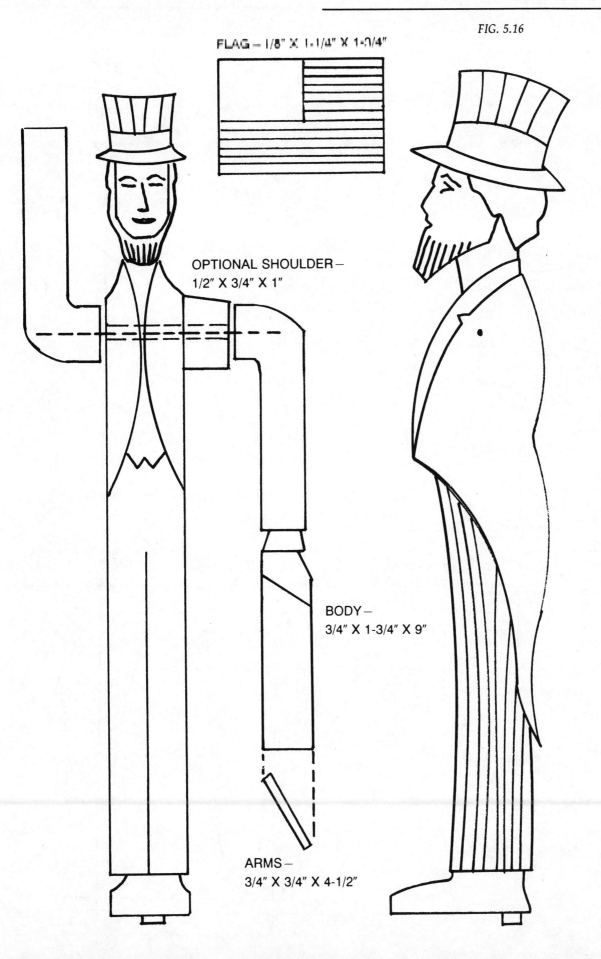

FLAG — 1/8" X 1-1/4" X 1-3/4"

OPTIONAL SHOULDER —
1/2" X 3/4" X 1"

BODY —
3/4" X 1-3/4" X 9"

ARMS —
3/4" X 3/4" X 4-1/2"

Gentleman Jim

FIG. 5.17

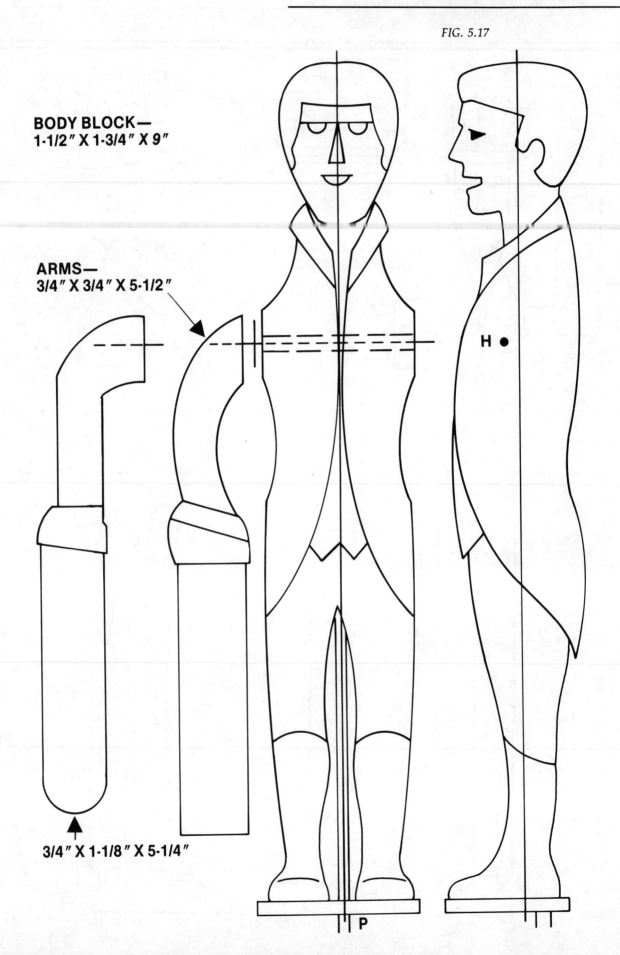

BODY BLOCK—
1-1/2″ X 1-3/4″ X 9″

ARMS—
3/4″ X 3/4″ X 5-1/2″

3/4″ X 1-1/8″ X 5-1/4″

H •

P

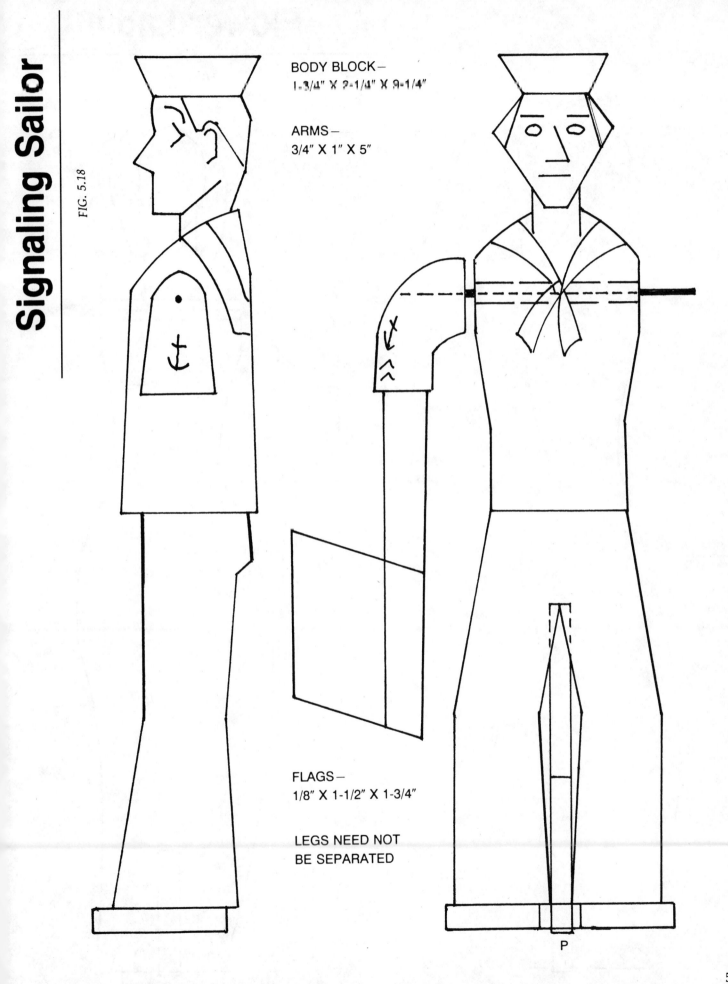

Signaling Sailor

FIG. 5.18

BODY BLOCK—
1-3/4" X 2-1/4" X 9-1/4"

ARMS—
3/4" X 1" X 5"

FLAGS—
1/8" X 1-1/2" X 1-3/4"

LEGS NEED NOT
BE SEPARATED

P

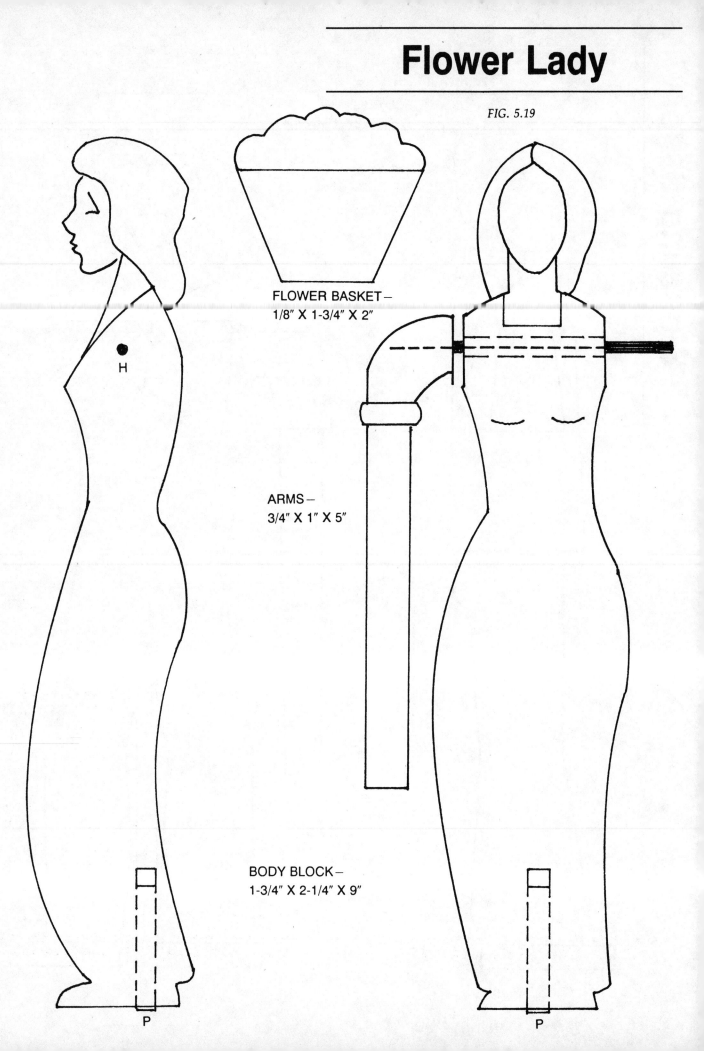

Flower Lady

FIG. 5.19

FLOWER BASKET—
1/8" X 1-3/4" X 2"

H

ARMS—
3/4" X 1" X 5"

BODY BLOCK—
1-3/4" X 2-1/4" X 9"

P

P

Colonial Dame

FIG. 5.20

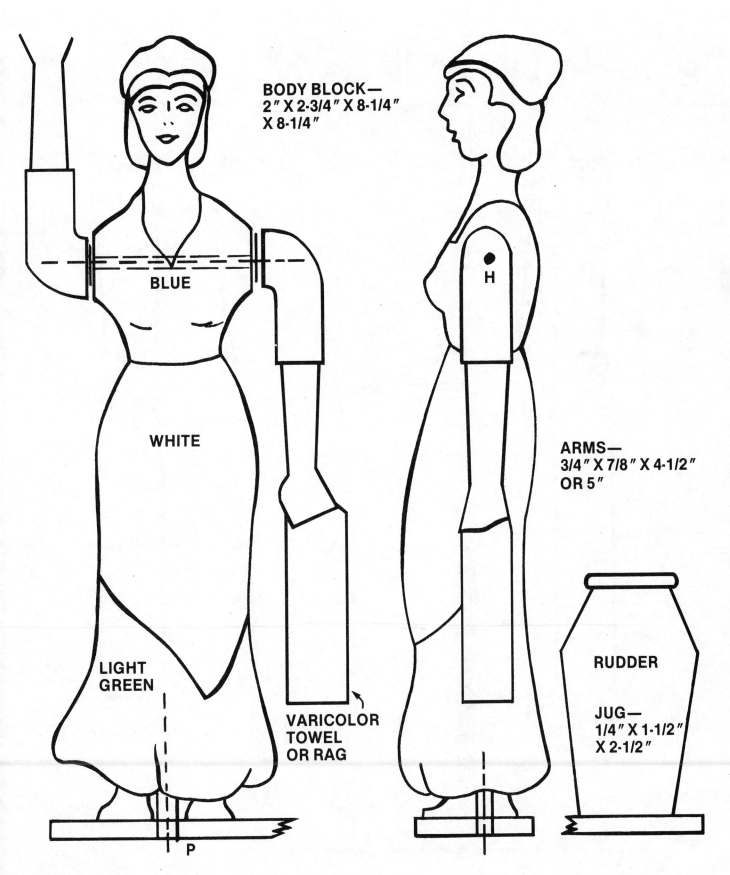

BODY BLOCK—
2″ X 2-3/4″ X 8-1/4″
X 8-1/4″

BLUE

WHITE

LIGHT
GREEN

VARICOLOR
TOWEL
OR RAG

P

H

ARMS—
3/4″ X 7/8″ X 4-1/2″
OR 5″

RUDDER

JUG—
1/4″ X 1-1/2″
X 2-1/2″

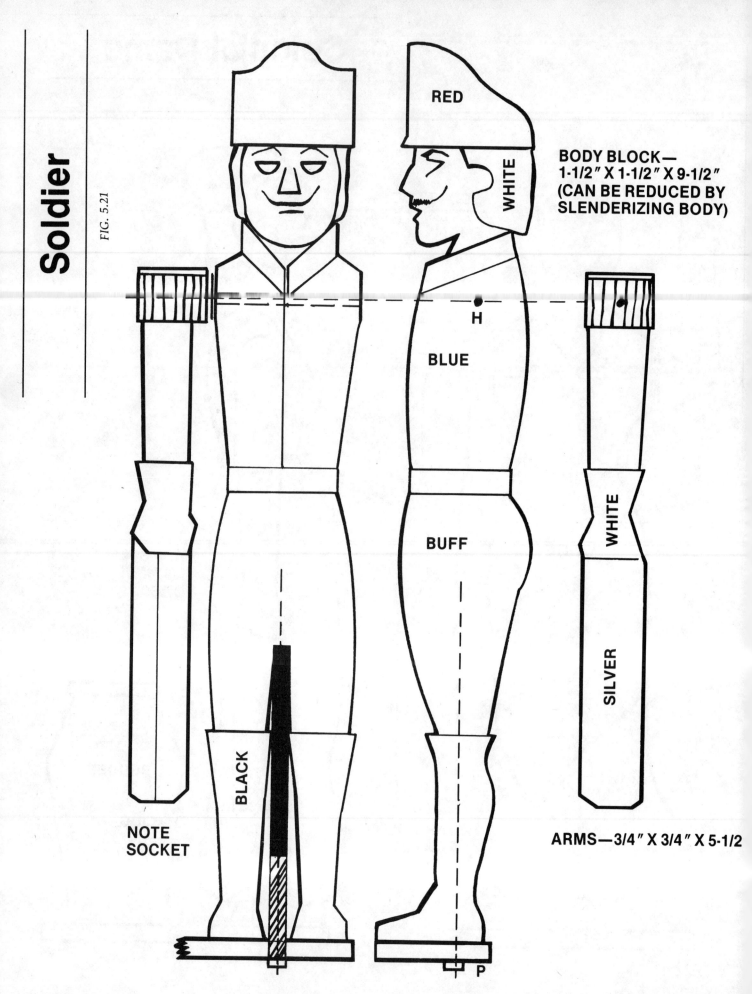

Soldier

FIG. 5.21

RED

WHITE

BODY BLOCK—
1-1/2″ X 1-1/2″ X 9-1/2″
(CAN BE REDUCED BY
SLENDERIZING BODY)

H

BLUE

BUFF

WHITE

SILVER

BLACK

NOTE
SOCKET

P

ARMS—3/4″ X 3/4″ X 5-1/2

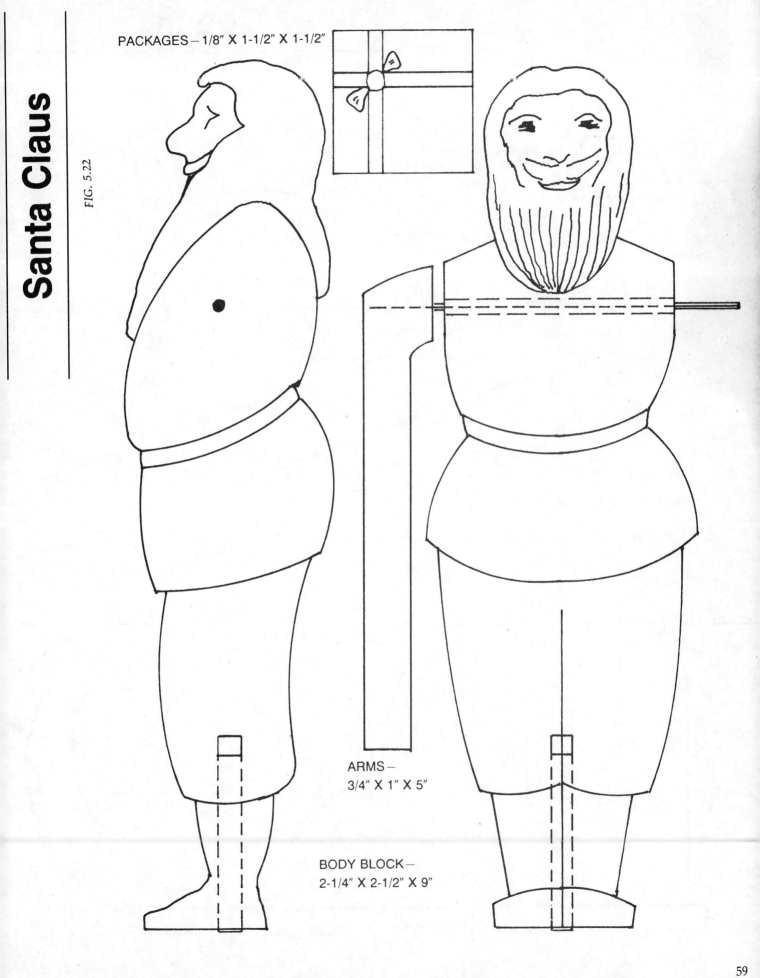

PACKAGES — 1/8" X 1-1/2" X 1-1/2"

ARMS —
3/4" X 1" X 5"

BODY BLOCK —
2-1/4" X 2-1/2" X 9"

Santa Claus

FIG. 5.22

Doggie

FIG. 5.23

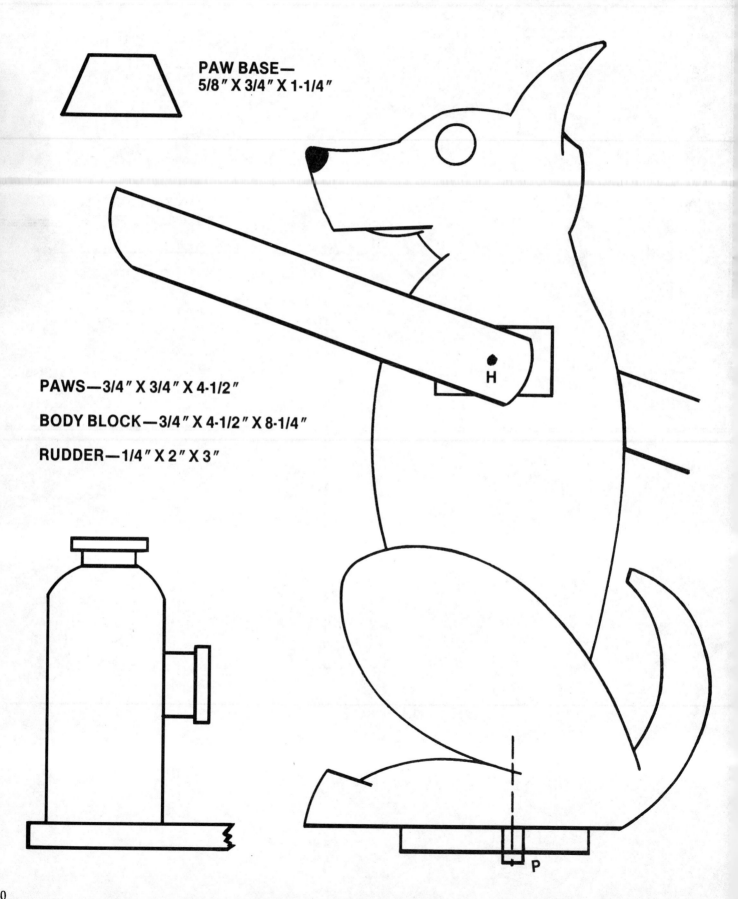

PAW BASE—
5/8″ X 3/4″ X 1-1/4″

PAWS—3/4″ X 3/4″ X 4-1/2″

BODY BLOCK—3/4″ X 4-1/2″ X 8-1/4″

RUDDER—1/4″ X 2″ X 3″

Man Rowing Boat

FIG. 5.24

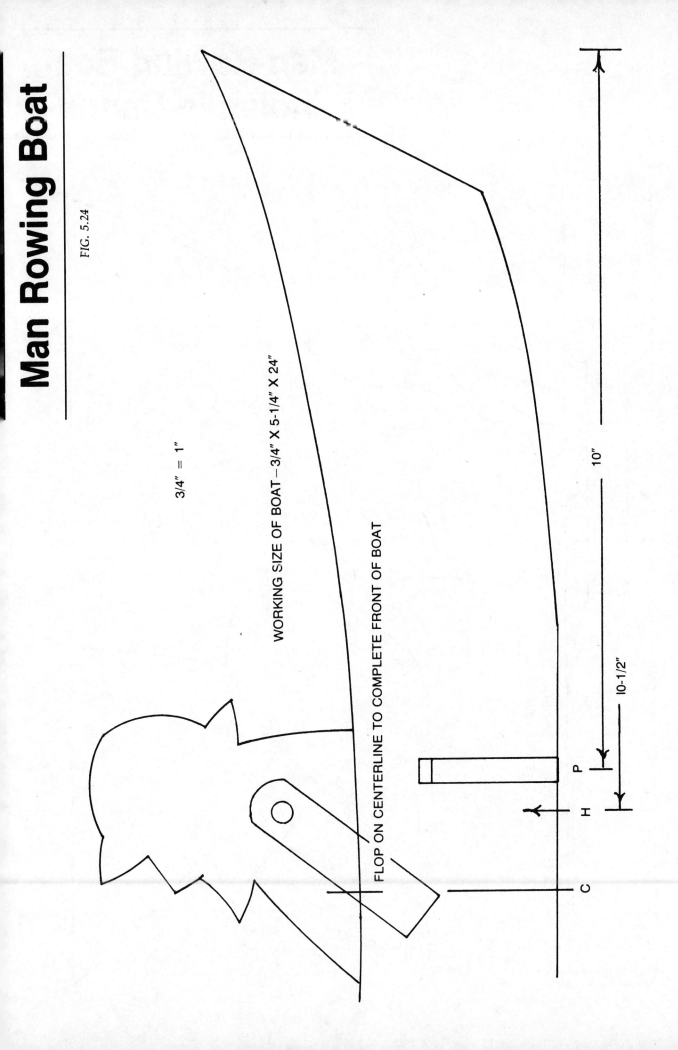

3/4" = 1"

WORKING SIZE OF BOAT — 3/4" X 5-1/4" X 24"

FLOP ON CENTERLINE TO COMPLETE FRONT OF BOAT

10"

10-1/2"

P

H

C

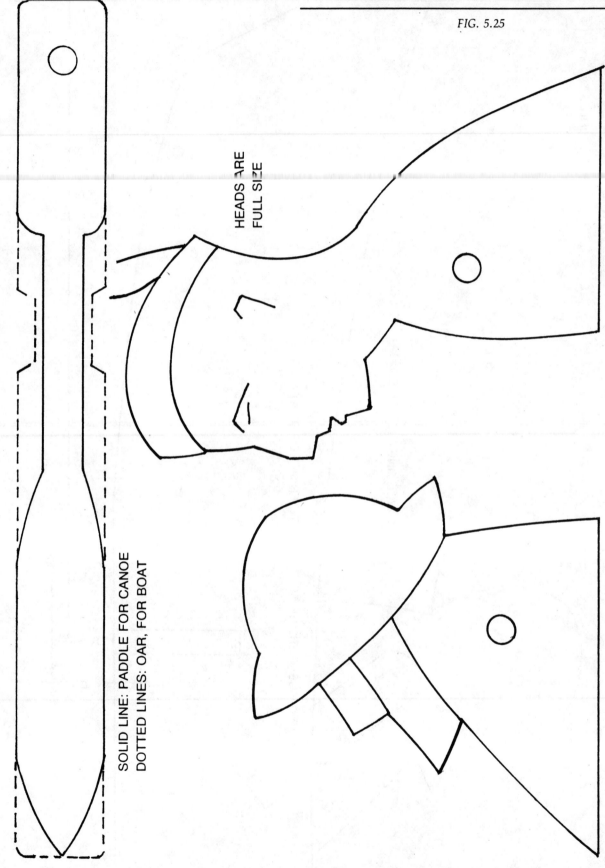

HEADS ARE FULL SIZE

SOLID LINE: PADDLE FOR CANOE
DOTTED LINES: OAR, FOR BOAT

Indian in Canoe

FIG. 5.26

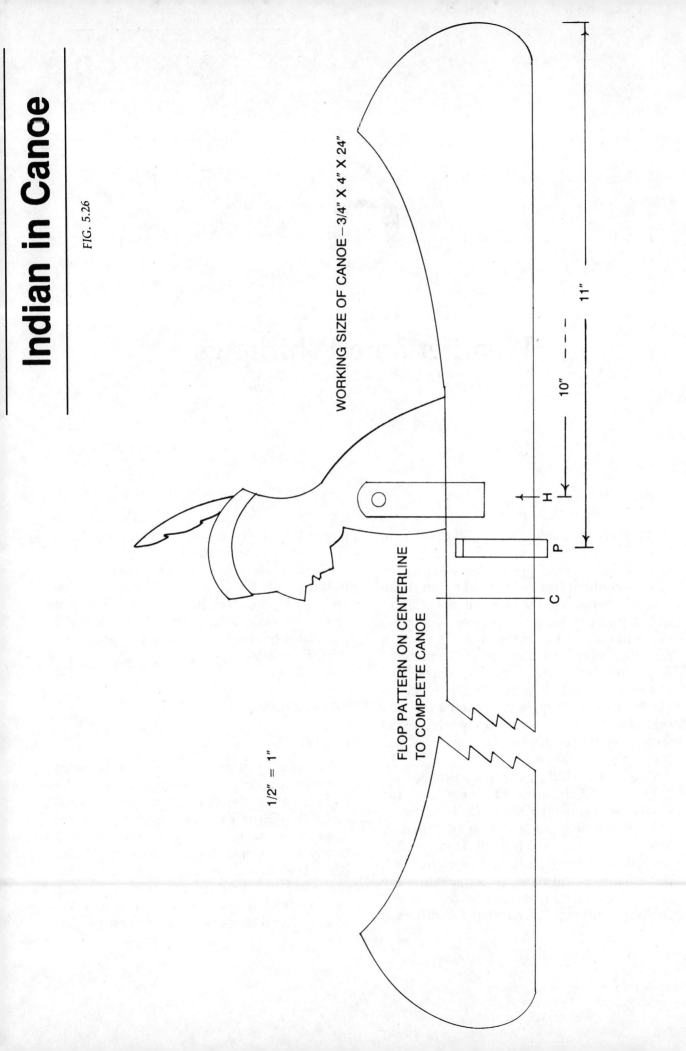

WORKING SIZE OF CANOE—3/4" X 4" X 24"

FLOP PATTERN ON CENTERLINE
TO COMPLETE CANOE

11"

10"

H

P

C

1/2" = 1"

6

Construction of
Weathervane Whirligigs

Weathervane models have been a prevalent form of whirligig in America. Essentially, they have two elements: They are vanes, and they have something turning or twirling on them, usually a propeller. The propeller may fulfill a design purpose, such as representing the sails of a windmill or the propeller of a ship, or it may be simply an added feature, something decorative and attention-getting. A whirligig maker may come up with a design which requires that the whirligig face into the wind. In that case, one has a weathervane whirligig of sorts, even if a conventional weathervane was the original intention.

One of my whirligigs was accepted for the 1986 Juried Exhibition of North Carolina Crafts, sponsored by the N.C. Museum of History in Raleigh. It is of a topsail schooner about 3 feet long and 2 feet tall. There are five propellers twirling on it; two of them move driveshafts, which cause passengers to wave things about. It can therefore be called a mechanical whirligig. But, as it has a spanker sail

that keeps it pointed into the wind, the ship is also a weathervane whirligig.

Weathervane types may be made small, as in the case of the Flying Witch and Georgine and Her Flying Machine. It is sometimes just as easy to make a large one. As soon as the principles of construction are grasped, anything is possible.

BASIC STEPS

Design

First of all, you must decide what you want to make as a vane, then draw it full-size. For some large weathervanes, I have glued several large sketch-pad pages together, or used newspaper sheets. When the paper won't fit on my drawing board, I pin it on the wall. This is good practice when designing large ones because you can stand back from your drawing and see it in perspective. I did this with the whale several times because my first proportions didn't seem just right. It is also advisable to use large felt-tipped pens when drawing the final lines, so you can see what you have. I have made codfish 2 feet long, whales 3 feet long, and a bathing beauty 4 feet long, and Halley's Comet, in this fashion. When you are designing smaller models you may need less paper but you will need to be more careful about getting the balance of the whirligig just right.

Patterns and Cuts

Make a pattern from the drawing and transfer it to the wood. For larger whirligigs, I usually cut out the drawings and use them as patterns. For silhouette models, the wood will be standard 1″ thick (milled ¾″). Weathervane types can also be sculpted in the round. My 24″ codfish was shaped like a fish and was 3″ thick. The fins were carved separately and inserted in ¼″ slots. When designing "in the round" weathervanes, remember that they should be streamlined. File and sand the completed body.

Balance and Pivot

Unlike other whirligigs, the position of the pivot point (P) for weathervane types is determined after the whirligig is completed. It can be estimated in planning but it should never be predetermined. If the propeller is small and light, point P can be found without having the propeller attached. If, however, the propeller is heavy and may be a weight factor, the propeller should be attached while determining the P position. Find the balance point (B) and mark it. Move forward on the vane and mark a point about halfway between the front end and B (Fig. 6.1). Ordinarily this could become the pivot point P. But some designs are back-heavy to begin with and P need only be a quarter of the distance forward to make the vane swing without putting a strain on the socket. If, after putting in a pivot socket, you should change your mind about the location, simply drill another socket hole in the new location.

The sockets for smaller whirligigs of this type can be the same as for other small whirligigs, like birds. Sockets can be drilled with a $\frac{7}{32}$″ bit and lined with $\frac{7}{32}$″ brass tubing, fitted with a cap. A 12d nail with head cut off can be a spindle. For larger whirligigs, a $\frac{3}{8}$″ tension pin, 2″ long, is a handy liner; this will take a 20d or 30d nail as a spindle. For longer and heavier vanes, a $\frac{5}{16}$″ or $\frac{3}{8}$″ socket can be drilled deeper and a ¼″ steel rod used as a spindle. If you get into heavier models, even larger sockets and rods will be required.

WEATHERVANE MODELS

Some of the larger whirligigs are not shown full-size in the illustrations. As the drawings are rather simple, there should be no problem with enlarging them. Except where instruct-

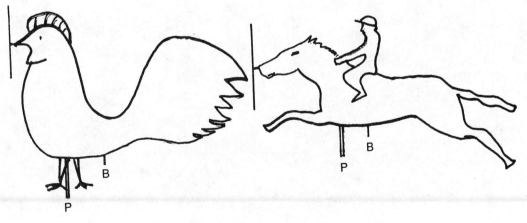

FIG. 6.1

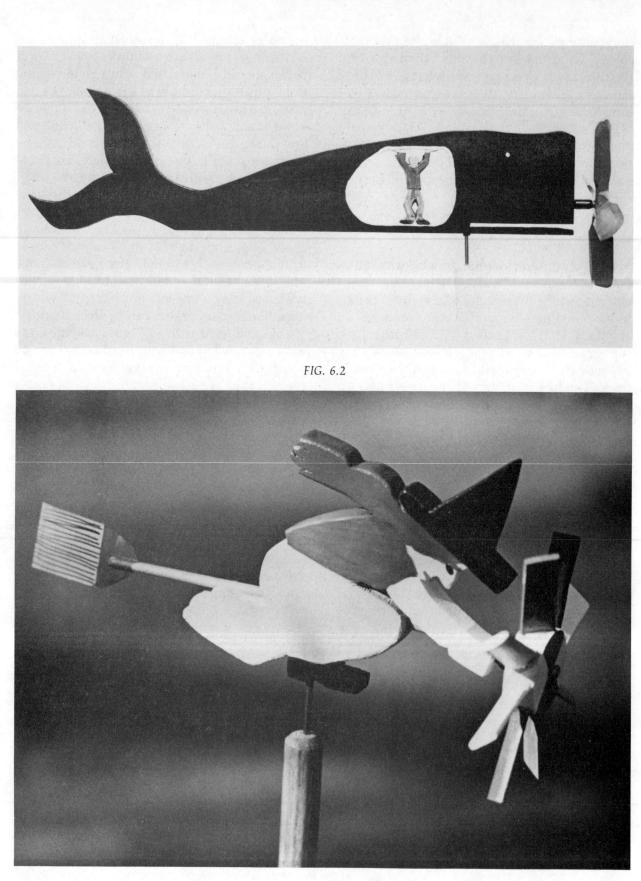

FIG. 6.2

FIG. 6.3

ed, do not predetermine the pivot point (P). Wait until you have the model completed; then find B and P.

Willy the Whale

MATERIALS
Whale body: $3/4'' \times 5'' \times 24''$
Socket liner: $3/8''$ tension pin, 2" long
Prop support: $5/8''$ dowel, 4" long
Propeller: four-bladed, with 4" blades

CONSTRUCTION
For the four-bladed prop, the $1\frac{1}{2}''$ square hub has a $3/16''$ sleeve tubing and is fastened with a $1\frac{1}{4}''$ No. 6 roundheaded screw and washers. If you prefer, a 6" double-bladed propeller will do, and it can be held with a nail.

While he may be made smaller or larger, I suggest that Willy be made 24" long and 5" high; the completed model is shown in Fig. 6.2. For this model, a $3/8''$ pivot socket was drilled 5 inches back from his nose, and a $5/8''$ hole for the propeller support was drilled $2\frac{1}{2}''$ from the front bottom edge. The main purpose of this support is to keep the blades from striking the body.

The Flying Witch

The Flying Witch in Fig. 6.3 was inspired by an antique whirligig I saw in the Museum of American Folk Art in New York City.

MATERIALS
Witch body block: $3/4'' \times 7'' \times 10''$ (see pattern)
Arms (2): $1/8'' \times 3/4'' \times 4''$ (see pattern)
Broomstick: $1/4''$ dowel, 12" long
Prop base: $1/2'' \times 1/2'' \times 1\frac{1}{2}''$
Broom: thin metal, $1\frac{1}{2}'' \times 2\frac{1}{2}''$

CONSTRUCTION
1. To make the witch, trace the pattern onto the wood block. Drill a $7/32''$ hole at P about 2" deep. Drill through the body with a $1/4''$ bit where the broomstick will go.
2. Cut out the propeller base and drill a $1/4''$ hole, $1/2''$ deep, at one end; glue the broomstick into it. Cut the end of it at an appropriate angle (as shown) and drill a small pilot hole for the hub screw. Cut a slot in the other end for the metal broom.
3. Glue the witch's arms to the body and propeller base and secure them with brads. Attach the metal broom.
4. A small, multibladed propeller was on the antique witch and will do nicely here.

Note that while the back of the witch's body could be sufficient to work as a vane, the broom end acts as a rudder and keeps her flying into the wind.

The Ships

Make the submarine and the ocean liner at least two feet long. As their silhouettes are relatively simple, drawing them in larger scale will not be difficult. The pivot point (P) for these whirligigs should not be marked until they have been completed with propellers and rudders in place.

SUBMARINE
The hull in the diagram measures $3/4'' \times 2\frac{1}{4}'' \times 24''$. The tower is added separately. The propeller may be of any relative size, and a special propeller support is not needed if the ends are rounded somewhat and the blades won't strike anything.

P is determined after the propeller is temporarily attached. The socket is a $3/8''$ socket, 2" deep, and a $3/4''$ tension pin is the liner.

OCEAN LINER
The hull and superstructure measures about $3/4'' \times 4\frac{1}{2}'' \times 24''$. The funnel and foremast will be added separately.

As in the case of the submarine, P will be determined after the propeller is in place.

To both models, a $1/4''$-thick rudder may be added at the stern to help "steer" the ships into the wind.

Georgine and Her Flying Machine

Georgine, shown in Fig. 6.4, was made for my neighbor, George, an old Navy pilot who still flies a small plane. But I thought the pilot should be a lady, so I called her Georgine! The

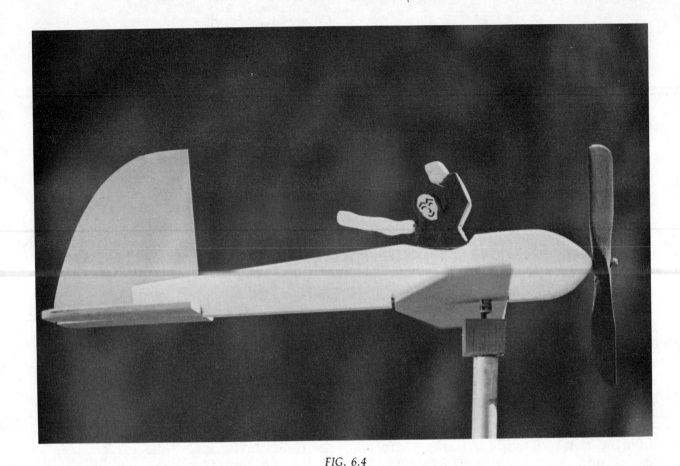

FIG. 6.4

airplane whirligig is one of the older ones of the 20th century, having been invented in the early days of aviation. Because all the drawings are not full-size, details are provided here.

MATERIALS
Fuselage: $\frac{3}{4}$" × $2\frac{1}{2}$" × 14"
Wing: $\frac{1}{4}$" × $3\frac{1}{2}$" × 14"
Stabilizer: $\frac{1}{4}$" × 4" × 6"
Pilot: $\frac{3}{4}$" × 2" × 3"
Scarf: $\frac{1}{4}$" × $\frac{1}{2}$" × 3"
Propeller: $\frac{3}{4}$" × $\frac{3}{4}$" × 6"
Tail (metal): $4\frac{1}{2}$" × $4\frac{1}{2}$"
Socket liner: $\frac{3}{8}$" tension pin, 2" long

CONSTRUCTION
1. Cut out the fuselage as indicated in the drawing, and shape it, rounding the top. Cut out a $\frac{1}{4}$" slot for the wing, beginning 3" from the nose of the plane and extending $3\frac{1}{2}$" toward the rear. Similarly, cut out the stabilizer slot, 2" in from the back

end. Cut the tail slot; if the tail is metal, this slot can be cut with a very thin saw blade, such as a coping saw. If a wood tail is preferred, cut the slot to permit a snug fit.

Lastly, drill a pilot hole in the nose for the screw that will hold the propeller in place. Sand the fuselage when all the cuts are made.

2. Make the wing from $\frac{1}{4}$" exterior plywood or any other thin piece of wood; shape it as indicated. Fit it into the fuselage wing slot, and secure it with glue and wire nails. Cut the stabilizer out of the same material and sand all sides round. Glue and nail it into the rear slot. Drill the pivot socket (P) through the wing and into the fuselage with a $\frac{3}{8}$" bit, allowing space for the metal cap. Insert the tension pin. The airplane can now be mounted on a stand with a 16d nail serving as a spindle.

3. Cut out the pilot piece and fit it into the

cockpit curve. Drill two $\frac{1}{4}''$ holes for the support dowel and the scarf. Cut out the rudder and glue or nail it in place.

4. Cut out and shape the propeller, after drilling the hub for $\frac{3}{16}''$ tubing. The airplane propeller will be somewhat slender, not shaped like a wing for a bird whirligig.

5. Finally, paint the airplane, the pilot, and the propeller separately. With dowel and glue, attach the pilot to the fuselage. Put the propeller in place with a 14" No. 6 roundheaded brass screw and washers.

Halley's Comet

If you want to make a whirligig that will be historic from the moment it is made and will be greatly admired if it is still around in 2062 when the celestial visitor returns, make Halley's Comet. There are many fascinating and imaginative pictures of Halley's and other comets to provide inspiration for a design.

If you create your own design, you can't be much further off than the artists who thought they saw comets resembling those in the illustrations. I have provided two models: both are drawn to the scale of $\frac{1}{4}'' = 1''$. One is taken from an old Aztec drawing of A.D. 1500, and the other is from a photograph of Halley's Comet taken in 1910. They are complete with tails caused by the solar winds. The propellers are appropriate because their blades can represent some of the ice particles spinning off.

AZTEC COMET

This design is constructed from a board $\frac{3}{4}''$ × 10" × 40". Because the tail will be quite heavy, the pivot point (P) need not be too far forward of the balance point (B). The tail can be carved out in the design shown, in which case it will be lighter. The socket is drilled with a $\frac{3}{8}''$ bit and a 2" tension pin serves as the liner. Use a 30d nail as a spindle.

MODERN COMET

The more realistic design is cut from a piece of wood $\frac{3}{4}''$ × 8" × 36". The socket and liner are the same as for the Aztec model.

The suggested propeller is a six-bladed model, made as illustrated. The circular hub has a 2" diameter, with a $\frac{3}{16}''$ hole in the center. Drill six $\frac{1}{4}''$ holes around the perimeter of the hub, 60 degrees apart. Cut six 5" lengths of $\frac{1}{4}''$ dowel; cut off half of the ends to a depth of $1\frac{1}{2}''$.

Make six vanes: 3" stars or 2" circles, $\frac{1}{8}''$ thick. Glue these vanes to the cut ends of the dowels. When dry, glue the dowels into the hub holes at 45-degree angles. The hub is

SUMMARY OF MATERIAL SIZES FOR WEATHERVANE WHIRLIGIGS
(in inches)

WOOD

Project	Body Block	Propellers
Willy the Whale	$\frac{3}{4}$ × 6 × 24	8" four-bladed
Flying Witch	$\frac{3}{4}$ × 7 × 10	4" multibladed
Submarine	$\frac{3}{4}$ × $2\frac{1}{4}$ × 24	Any type
Ocean Liner	$\frac{3}{4}$ × $4\frac{1}{2}$ × 24	Any type
Georgine	$\frac{3}{4}$ × $2\frac{1}{2}$ × 14	6" twin-bladed
Aztec Comet	$\frac{3}{4}$ × 10 × 40	See drawing
Halley's Comet	$\frac{3}{4}$ × 8 × 36	See drawing

OTHER MATERIALS

Project	Propeller Sleeves	Socket Liners	Spindles
Witch	$\frac{3}{16}$ brass tubing	$\frac{7}{32}$ tubing	16d nail
Georgine	$\frac{3}{16}$ brass tubing	$\frac{7}{32}$ tubing	16d nail
All others	$\frac{3}{16}$ brass tubing	$\frac{3}{8}$ tension pin, 2"	20d–30d nail

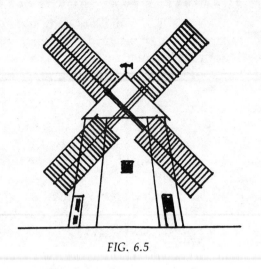

FIG. 6.5

mos shining blueish through the tail. Any color will do for a whirligig comet.

Another favorite type of whirligig in the weathervane category is the windmill (Fig. 6.5). In 1980, the U.S. Postal Service issued four commemorative stamps celebrating 300 years of windmills in this country. The oldest portrayed still stands on Cape Cod in Eastham, Massachusetts. It was built entirely of wood in 1630 in Plymouth and transported around a bit before it was finally moved to Eastham, where it's become an attraction for summer visitors to the Cape Cod National Seashore. Windmill whirligigs are fun to make and can also be a challenge if the builder wants to make a model with real vanes and cloth sails. While operating windmills have to be turned to have the vanes face the wind, windmill whirligigs have rudders attached for doing that job.

lined with $\frac{3}{16}$" tubing and is fitted to the nucleus of the comet with a $1\frac{1}{2}$" No. 6 roundheaded screw.

Painting the comets can be a work of total imagination, as even astronomers are not sure of all their characteristics. The Aztec comet is pictured as being a yellow star, with a light blue tail; the 1910 comet is white, with the cos-

Willy the Whale

FIG. 6.6

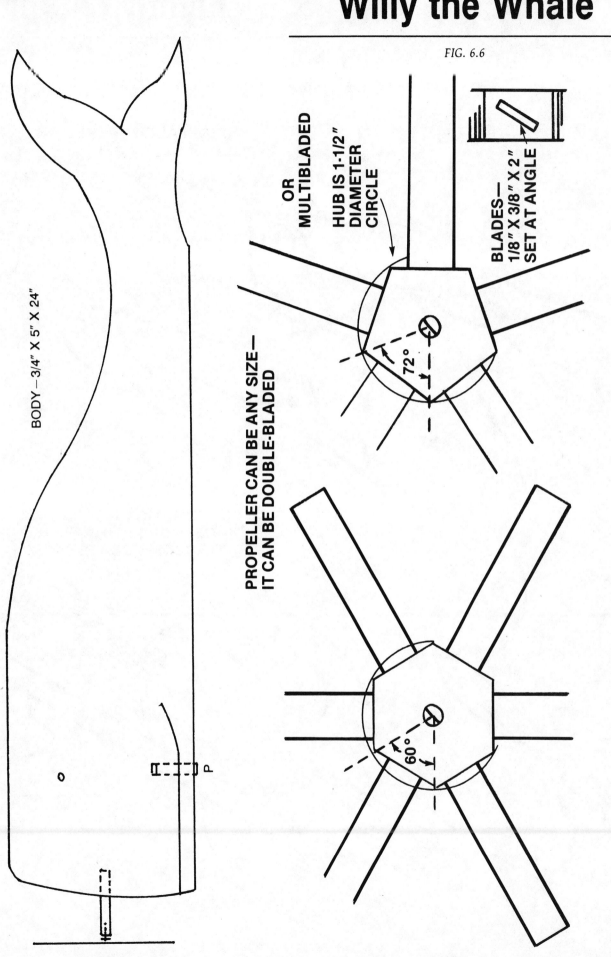

BODY—3/4" X 5" X 24"

O

P

OR
MULTIBLADED

HUB IS 1-1/2"
DIAMETER
CIRCLE

BLADES—
1/8" X 3/8" X 2"
SET AT ANGLE

72°

PROPELLER CAN BE ANY SIZE—
IT CAN BE DOUBLE-BLADED

60°

Flying Witch

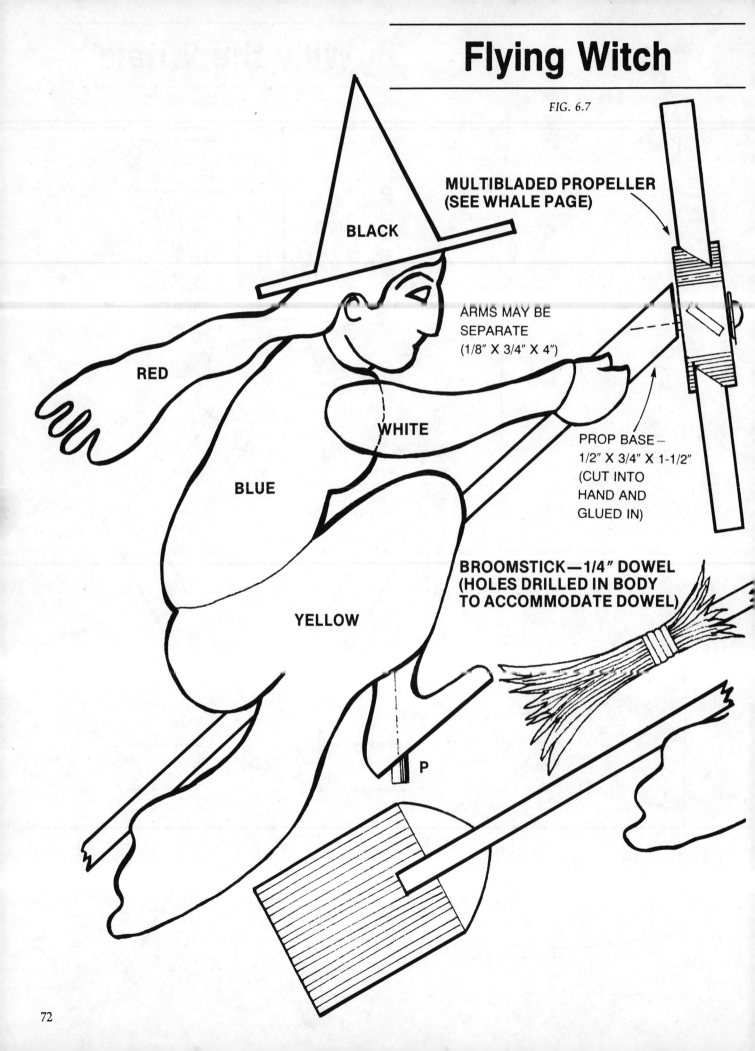

FIG. 6.7

MULTIBLADED PROPELLER (SEE WHALE PAGE)

BLACK

ARMS MAY BE SEPARATE (1/8" X 3/4" X 4")

RED

WHITE

PROP BASE— 1/2" X 3/4" X 1-1/2" (CUT INTO HAND AND GLUED IN)

BLUE

BROOMSTICK—1/4" DOWEL (HOLES DRILLED IN BODY TO ACCOMMODATE DOWEL)

YELLOW

P

FIG. 6.8

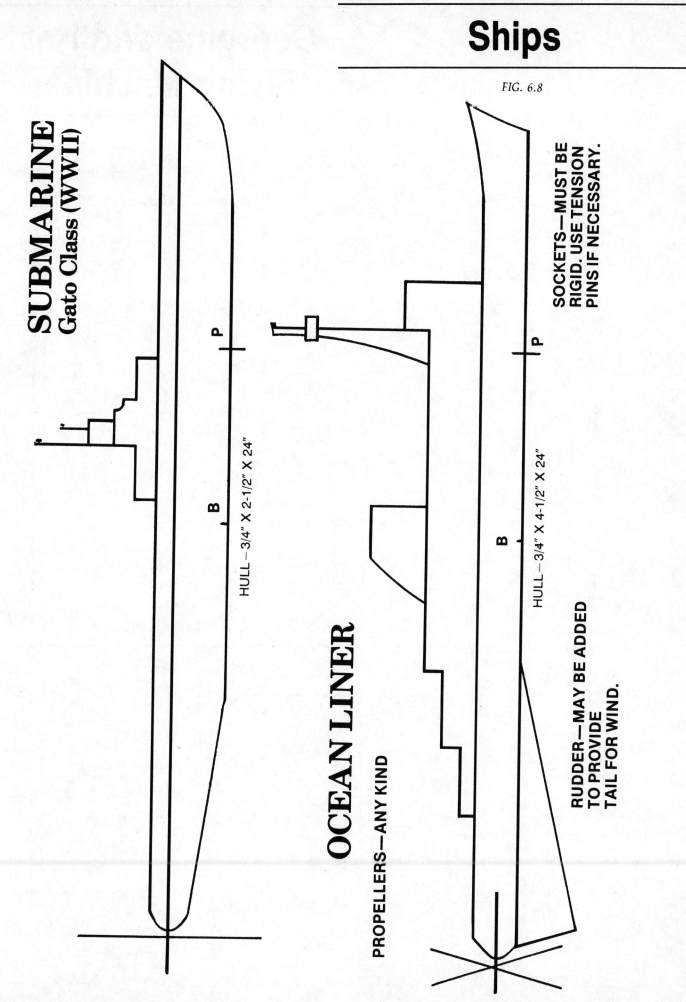

SUBMARINE
Gato Class (WWII)

HULL — 3/4" X 2-1/2" X 24"

P

B

OCEAN LINER

PROPELLERS—ANY KIND

HULL — 3/4" X 4-1/2" X 24"

P

B

SOCKETS—MUST BE RIGID. USE TENSION PINS IF NECESSARY.

RUDDER—MAY BE ADDED TO PROVIDE TAIL FOR WIND.

FIG. 6.9

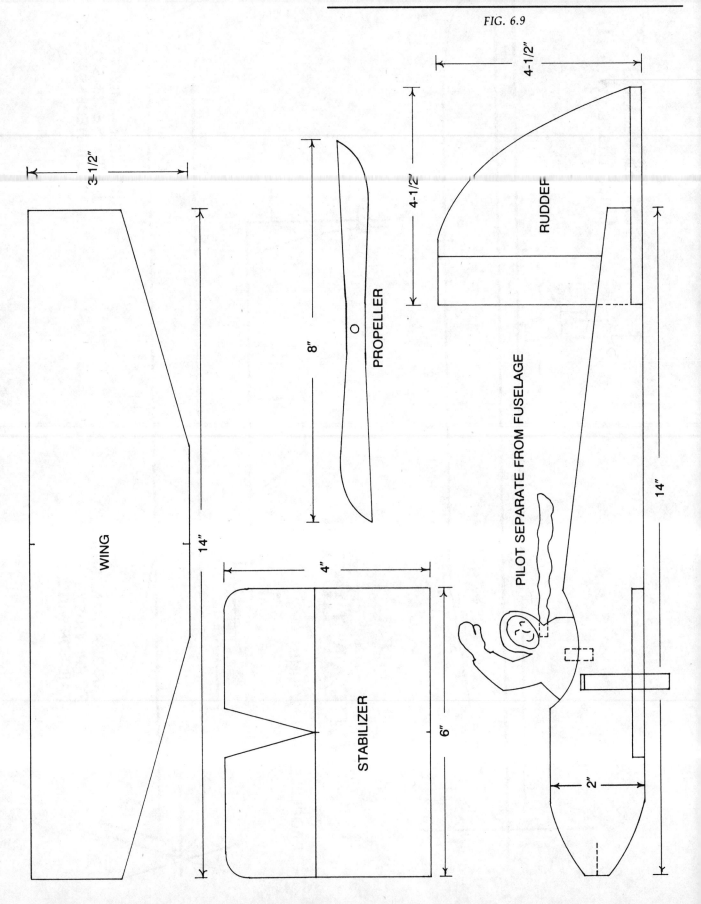

4-1/2"

3-1/2"

4-1/2

RUDDER

PROPELLER

8"

14"

WING

PILOT SEPARATE FROM FUSELAGE

14"

4"

STABILIZER

6"

2"

Comets

FIG. 6.10

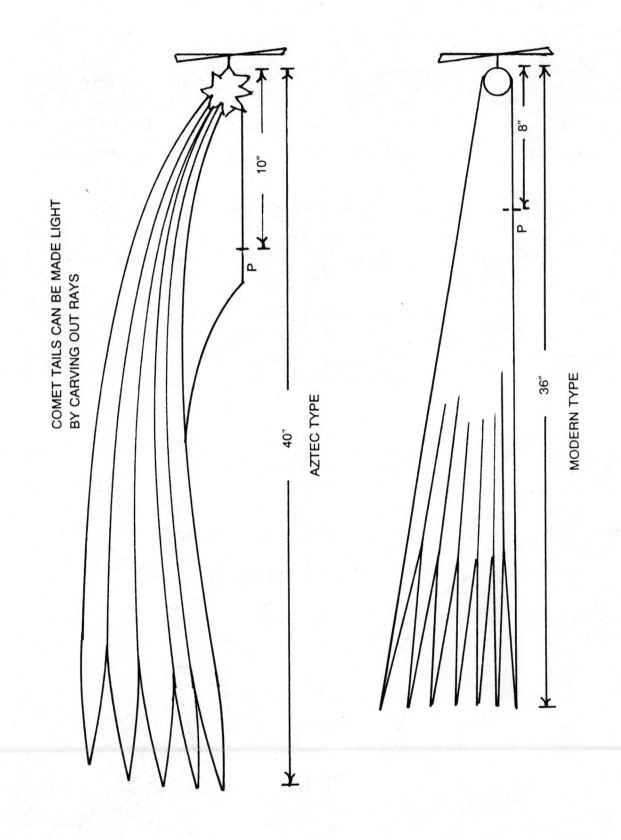

COMET TAILS CAN BE MADE LIGHT
BY CARVING OUT RAYS

10"

P

40"

AZTEC TYPE

8"

P

36"

MODERN TYPE

Comet Propeller

FIG. 6.11

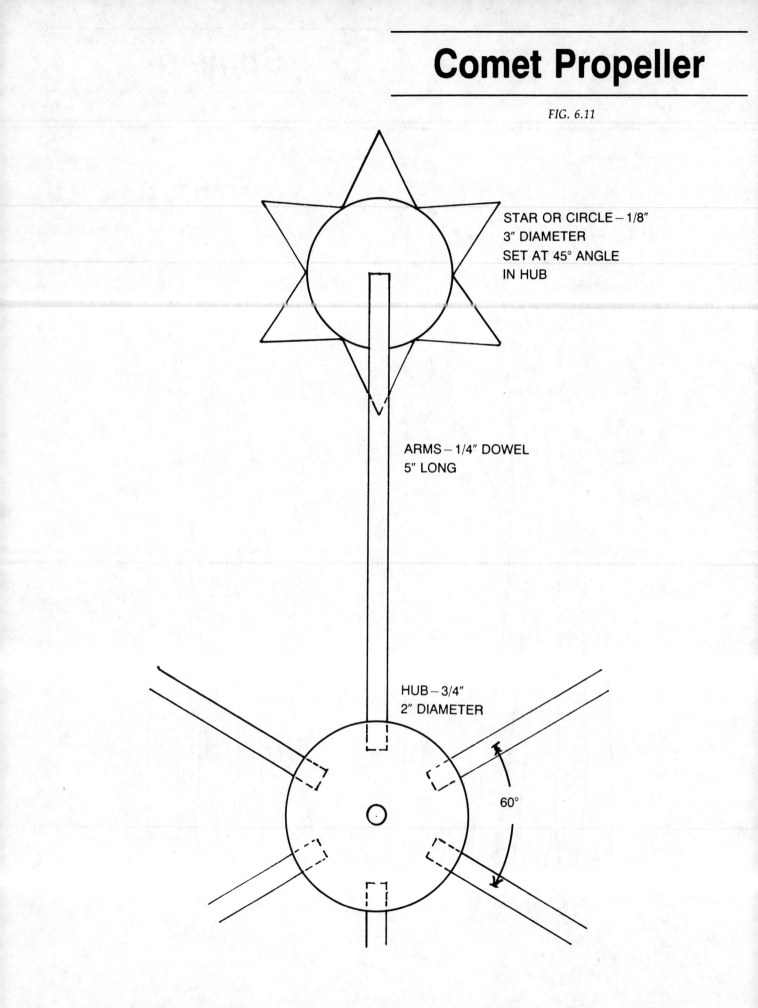

STAR OR CIRCLE – 1/8"
3" DIAMETER
SET AT 45° ANGLE
IN HUB

ARMS – 1/4" DOWEL
5" LONG

HUB – 3/4"
2" DIAMETER

60°

7

Construction of Mechanical Whirligigs

Mechanical whirligigs change the rotary motion of a wind propeller to vertical or horizontal motion. These movements, usually transferred to figures or objects by connecting rods or wires, activate them. Woodsmen chop or saw wood, mules kick, chicken feed, women milk cows or churn butter, and so forth. Most mechanical whirligigs are relatively simple to make once the design has been developed and the mechanism tested. On the other hand, new and experimental ideas take many hours to perfect. Camshafts have to be bent just right, and they have to be seated in steady brackets or supports. The proper length of connecting rods has to be determined. Designed figures may not move quite as planned. I once drew a design of a blacksmith hammering away on an anvil, but the whirligig didn't work. The arm needed more lift than the design provided, and the problem could not readily be adjusted. The experience convinced me that, indeed, trial and error is the principal method used by mechanical whirligig creators.

BASIC STEPS

The development of a new design can be seen as a series of seven steps.

1. *Make a drawing to scale.* The first drawing will probably be a rough sketch, but sooner or later this will have to be changed to something measurable.

   In this sketch, draw the type of power shaft you intend to use, and show how the circular movement of the propeller will drive whatever movement is expected of the objects on the platform or base. Also, draw the figures or objects and show how connecting rods will move them. Some parts will require full-size drawings.

2. *Cut out all parts.* Some complete units, like propellers, can be assembled and painted at this point. Large mechanical propellers are difficult to paint when bolted or welded in their final position.

3. *Construct the frame.* The frame consists of the main post on which the whirligig—or

FIG. 7.1

4. *Mark off and locate where the driveshaft or connecting rods will pass through the frame, and mark the positions of the figures.* Drill the necessary holes and put the driveshaft or camshaft in position. The propeller may be temporarily seated, and the gears or wheels added. The entire power assembly can be rotated to make certain that it works correctly.

5. *Place the figures on the frame.* Put the connecting rods in place and turn the driveshaft to see how it all works. When all the parts operate as they should, secure all pieces permanently with glue and nails, or screws.

6. *Add the rudder.* Secure it with one or two finishing nails through the base.

7. *Secure the propeller.* The size of the propeller will be determined by the size of the whirligig and the power necessary to move the objects or figures.

Mechanical whirligigs of some complexity will, of course, require additional procedures, but the steps listed above provide a good general outline of construction for most of the simpler types.

INDIVIDUAL MODELS

The Churning Woman

The Churning Woman whirligig shown in Fig. 7.1 has been around in America for a long time, and many adaptations of it have been made. A half-size diagram of a working model (scale: $\frac{1}{2}'' = 1''$) and other detailed full-scale drawings are given in this chapter.

MATERIALS

The list of parts for the Churning Woman whirligig includes the following:
a. Post: $1\frac{1}{2}'' \times 1\frac{1}{2}'' \times 13''$
b. Base: $\frac{3}{4}'' \times 2'' \times 10''$
c. Block: $\frac{3}{4}'' \times \frac{3}{4}'' \times 2''$
d. Sleeve: $\frac{5}{8}'' \times 4\frac{1}{2}''$ (old curtain rod)
e. Driveshaft: $\frac{1}{4}''$ carriage bolt, 6" long
f. Washer: for $\frac{1}{4}''$ bolt
g. Wheel: $\frac{1}{2}'' \times 2''$ in diameter (can be any shape)

the body of the whirligig, if this is the case — pivots, and the platform or base on which the action takes place. The frame will also include the pivot socket because it is advisable to have the whirligig in an upright position on a stand while working on it. Some large frames will have to be secured in a vise, but even then it is best to have the pivot socket made before other parts are added.

The socket hole may have to be drilled in a special support bracket under the platform. The position of the socket support will be determined by the relation of the balance point (B) and the pivot point (P), as in the case of the weathervane whirligigs. The socket and spindle should be large enough to support the weight of the whirligig. For the ones illustrated here, a $\frac{3}{8}''$ socket with a 2" tension pin should be sufficient. Or, if a long spindle is contemplated, a $\frac{5}{16}''$ socket will hold a $\frac{1}{4}''$ steel rod.

78

FIG. 7.2

h. Screw: ¾″ roundheaded
i. Connecting rod: stiff wire
j. Yoke: ¼″ × ¼″ × 3″
k. Churn: 1½″ round, 2¾″ (or 3″) high
l. Arms: 2½″ between yoke and arm screw (½″)
m. Figure: 2″ × 5″ overall
n. Rudder: 4″ × 7″ overall
o. Socket: ⅜″ tension pin, 2″ long

CONSTRUCTION

1. *Frame.* This is the basic structure consisting of post (a), stand or base (b) and socket (o), with socket liner. Place the frame on a mounting stand.
2. *Power mechanism.* These are items (d) through (h) which constitute the elements in the transfer of power from the propeller. The propeller can be added when everything else is completed.
3. *Moving and Related Parts.* These include the yoke (j), churn (k), figure (m), and arms (l). A ½″ roundhead No. 4 screw holds the arms to the body. The parts are assembled and tested for permanent positioning with connecting rod or wire (i).
4. *Rudder.* The tail or rudder is secured last. A nail through the base will hold it firm.

Signaling Trainman

The Signaling Trainman, shown in Fig. 7.2, has the same power mechanism as Churning Woman, except that it is located below the base rather than above it. This means that a slot ½″ × 1½″ must be cut into the base to per-

FIG. 7.3

mit the connecting rod to pass through. The location of the slot must be planned at the time the power mechanism is fitted, and the cut should be made before any parts are attached to the frame.

The trainman is waving his red signal flag and his lantern in an attempt to stop the onrushing train, which is headed for a pile of rocks on the track. The technical drawing of the whole whirligig is half size ($\frac{1}{2}$" = 1"), while the separate drawings of the trainman and the propeller are full scale.

The body of the trainman is cut into so the arms can be positioned in the slot. The hub of the arms has a short piece of $\frac{5}{32}$" tubing in it to enable the arms to move freely. The connecting rod can be made of any stiff wire. The same type of rod serves as the arm axle. The pile of stones can be real pebbles, glued together, or the rock pile can be carved of wood.

The same power mechanism can be used for many kinds of whirligig movements. Recently I saw the same type of mechanism on a mar-
80

velous whirligig from Jugtown, North Carolina, an area famous for its native pottery. Instead of churning butter or waving a flag, a figure was making a pot, a small, ceramic replica of a real Jugtown product. All parts except the pot and drive shaft were made of wood.

Forever Grinding

This man eternally sharpening his scythe while his wife turns the grindstone (Fig. 7.3) is an old whirligig idea, possibly with origins in Scandinavia. Some have been made more realistic by having the characters dressed up in cloth. There is only one cam to make in the $\frac{1}{8}$" driveshaft and the rest is easy.

MATERIALS
Platform: $\frac{3}{4}$" × 8" x 13"
Pivot base: $1\frac{1}{2}$" × $1\frac{1}{2}$" × 2"
Shaft stanchions (3): $\frac{3}{4}$" × $2\frac{1}{2}$" × $3\frac{1}{2}$"
Grindstone: $\frac{3}{4}$" × 3" diameter
Water trough: $1\frac{1}{8}$" × $1\frac{3}{4}$" × 3"
Man's body: $\frac{3}{4}$" × 3" × 7"
   arms: $\frac{1}{2}$" × $1\frac{1}{2}$" × 3"
Scythe blade: $\frac{1}{8}$" × $\frac{3}{4}$" × 3"
Woman's top: $1\frac{1}{4}$" × $1\frac{1}{4}$" × $4\frac{1}{4}$"
   bottom: $\frac{3}{4}$" × 2" × $2\frac{3}{4}$"
   arms: $\frac{1}{8}$" × $\frac{3}{4}$" × $2\frac{3}{4}$"
Socket liner: $\frac{3}{8}$" tension pin, 2" long
Stanchion tubing: $\frac{7}{8}$" brass tubing, or other
Driveshaft: $\frac{1}{8}$" steel rod, 16" long
Propeller hub: $1\frac{1}{2}$" × 2" × 2"
   blades (2): $\frac{1}{4}$" × $3\frac{1}{2}$" × $6\frac{1}{2}$"
Tail: sheet metal, 4" × 5"

PLATFORM
Cut out the base, draw the centerline on top and bottom, and mark the location of each object on it (man, woman, stanchions). Cut the tail slot with a coping saw. Drill the screw holes. Then make the support block or pivot base, drilling it with a $\frac{3}{8}$" bit for the tension pin. Glue and nail it in place; add the tension pin and cap. Make the stanchions; make sure the driveshaft holes will be the same height above the platform when in position. The recommended bit size is $\frac{7}{32}$" or $\frac{1}{4}$" to allow for a sleeve or liner of metal tubing. Temporarily

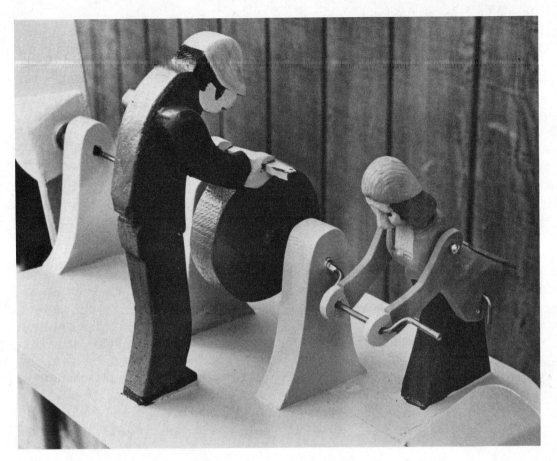

FIG. 7.4

put the end stanchions in place first, then align the middle stanchion with tubing or rod in place. Usually some adjustments have to be made with the center hole. When the alignment is correct, fasten the front two stanchions in place.

DRIVESHAFT

Thread the ⅛" rod 1¾" from the front end. Make a ½" deep cam 1½"wide beginning at 11¾" from that end. The camshaft is now complete. Make the grindstone, drilling a small hole at the center. First, slide the third stanchion along the shaft, followed by the grindstone. Then put the shaft in the other stanchions and glue the third stanchion in place. The grindstone should be secured with adhesive in the middle of the last two stanchions. Glue the water trough in place after cutting it down to keep the grindstone moving freely. This piece is only for show, not to tie up the works.

FIGURES

Cut out the man and hold him in place; mark out the proper position of his arms. Secure them to the body with brads and glue, and set the man in final position with a screw and glue. Attach the scythe blade. Finish the woman's parts; the torso will require some carving. The bottom part may be reinforced with a metal sleeve to hold the joint steady. A small rod (¹⁄₁₆" or ³⁄₃₂") will be the axle. Put the parts together and test the woman's movements with the driveshaft turning. The arms may have to be placed in the driveshaft before being attached to the body with a ¾" No. 4 roundheaded screw. When all is in order, secure the woman to the platform. Fig. 7.4 provides a closeup of the two figures in position, working away.

PROPELLER

The suggested propeller is double-bladed, 14" diameter. It can be screwed on the drive-

81

shaft with glue and be secured with $^6/_{32}$" machine nuts. Enough washers must be added to keep the grindstone and the woman's hands in the right place, as well as to keep the propeller from striking the base. Wooden beads between metal washers work well, if filling space on the driveshaft is a problem. The tail can be made into any shape and slipped into the rear slot. It need not be above the platform; some tails on whirligigs of this sort are below or partly below the base line.

Power may also be transferred by means of cogs, gears, belts and any of many other easily found mechanically functioning parts. Or it need not be transferred at all. Many old whirligigs were constructed with a direct drive mechanism of the type shown in Fig. 7.5. Strong supports are needed for the driveshaft or camshaft.

A warning should be issued here: A craftsperson who becomes interested in this simple and inexpensive machinery will never be quite the same. All kinds of ideas for making things

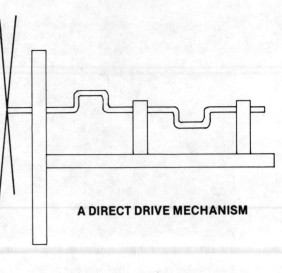

A DIRECT DRIVE MECHANISM

FIG. 7.5

work from the wind will constantly pop into the head, and at odd moments when one sits with pencil and paper in hand, a new design for something funny and fascinating will make its appearance.

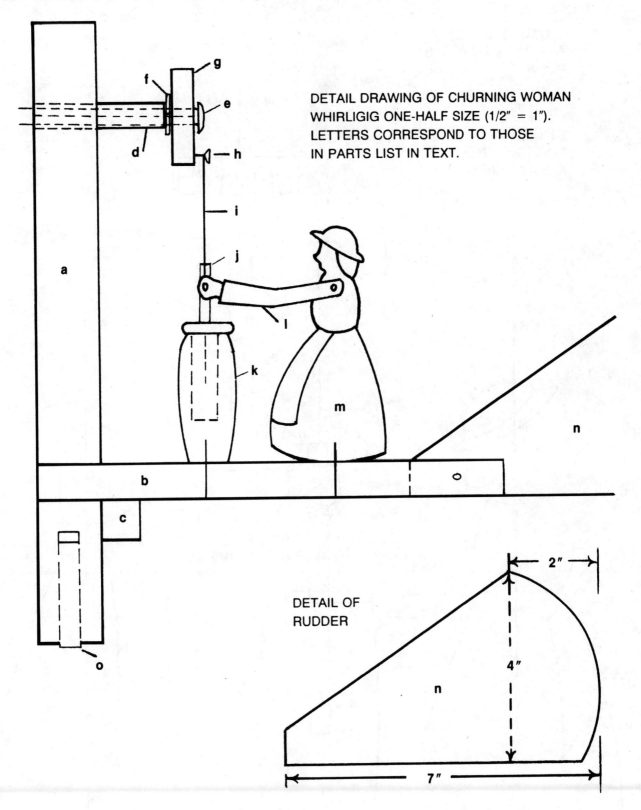

DETAIL DRAWING OF CHURNING WOMAN
WHIRLIGIG ONE-HALF SIZE (1/2″ = 1″).
LETTERS CORRESPOND TO THOSE
IN PARTS LIST IN TEXT.

DETAIL OF
RUDDER

2″

4″

n

7″

FIG. 7.6

83

Churning Woman

FIG. 7.7

WOMAN BLOCK
A—3/4″ X 2-1/4″ X 5″
B—3/4″ X 2″ X 5-1/2″

CHURN—
1-1/2″ ROUND
X 2-3/4″ HIGH

Full-size detail

YOKE—1/4″ X 3/4″ X 3″

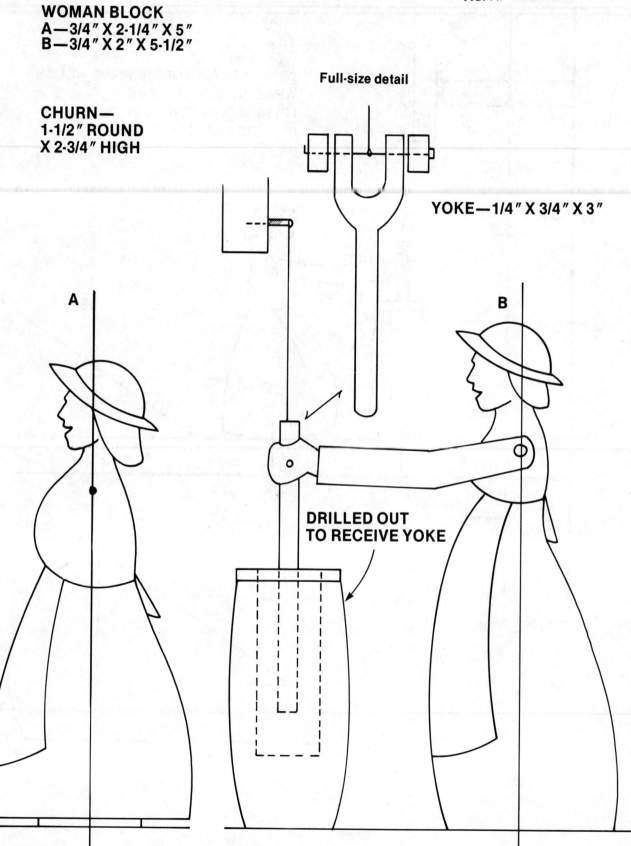

A

B

DRILLED OUT
TO RECEIVE YOKE

Signaling Trainman

FIG. 7.8

One-half size (1/2″ = 1″)

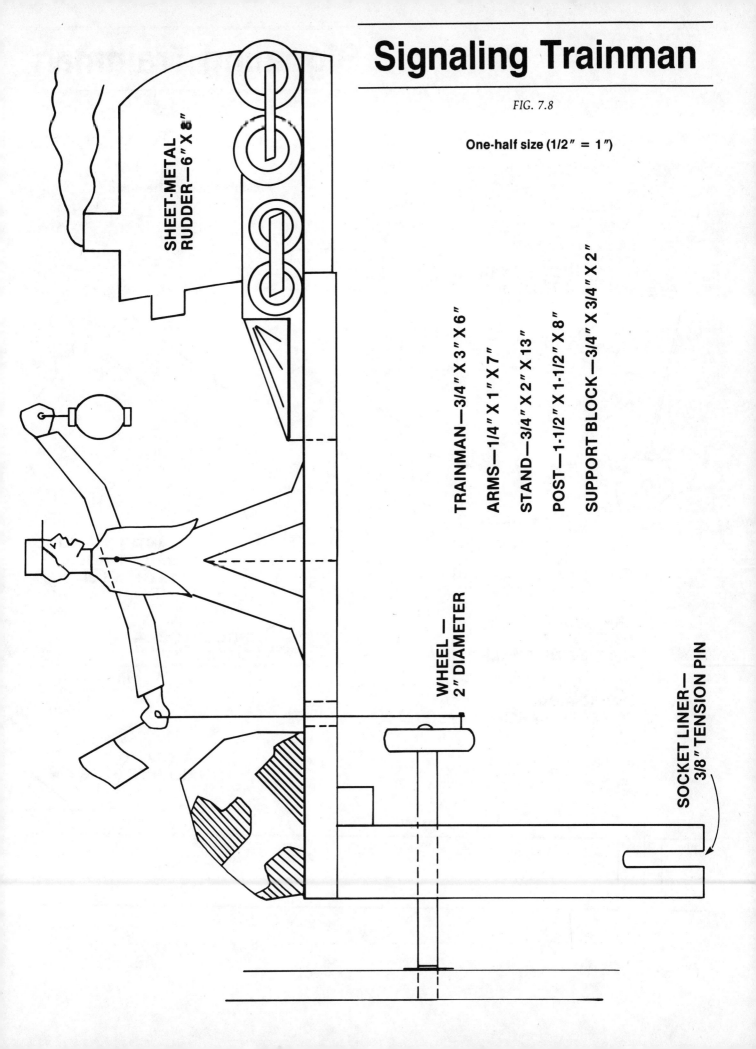

SHEET-METAL RUDDER—6″ X 8″

TRAINMAN—3/4″ X 3″ X 6″

ARMS—1/4″ X 1″ X 7″

STAND—3/4″ X 2″ X 13″

POST—1-1/2″ X 1-1/2″ X 8″

SUPPORT BLOCK—3/4″ X 3/4″ X 2″

WHEEL — 2″ DIAMETER

SOCKET LINER— 3/8″ TENSION PIN

Signaling Trainman

FIG. 7.9

Full-size detail of Trainman

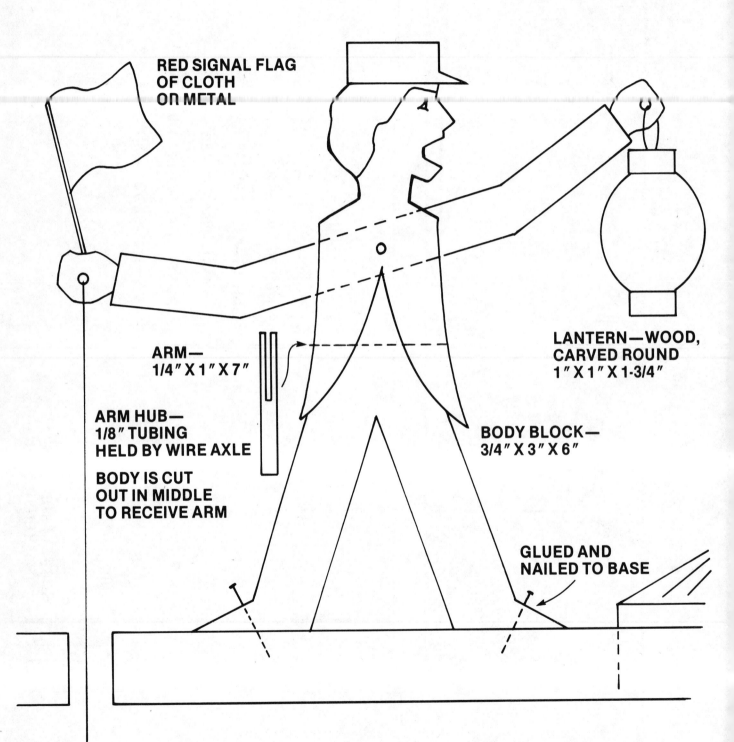

RED SIGNAL FLAG
OF CLOTH
ON METAL

ARM—
1/4″ X 1″ X 7″

ARM HUB—
1/8″ TUBING
HELD BY WIRE AXLE

BODY IS CUT
OUT IN MIDDLE
TO RECEIVE ARM

LANTERN—WOOD,
CARVED ROUND
1″ X 1″ X 1-3/4″

BODY BLOCK—
3/4″ X 3″ X 6″

GLUED AND
NAILED TO BASE

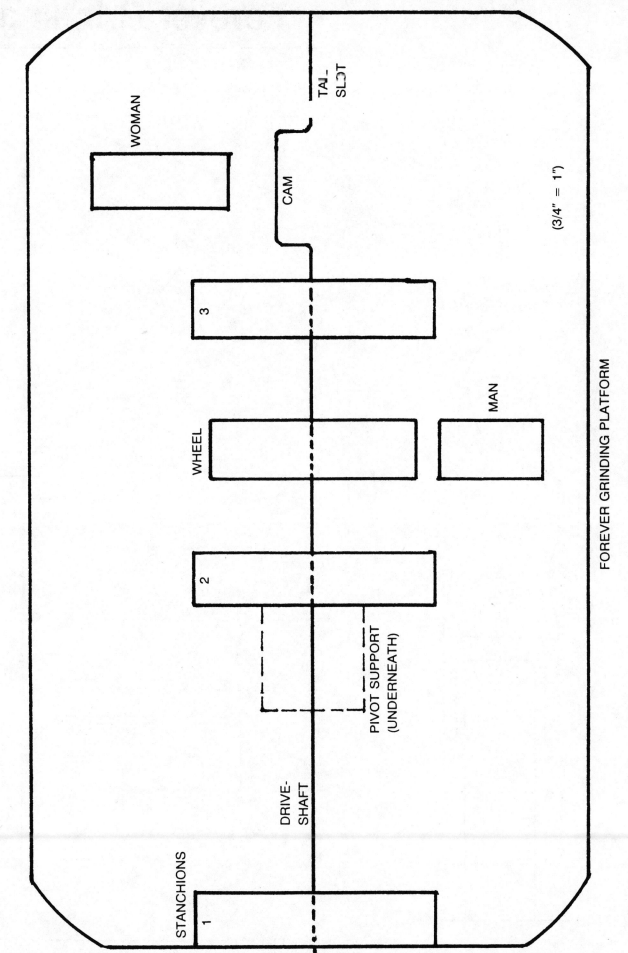

FOREVER GRINDING PLATFORM

FIG. 7.10

Forever Grinding

FIG. 7.11

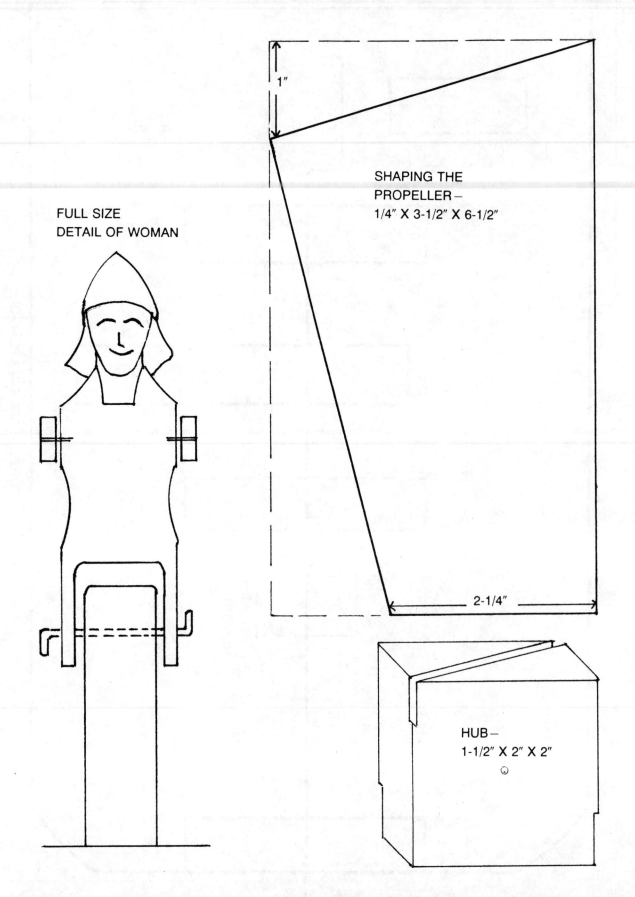

FULL SIZE
DETAIL OF WOMAN

1"

SHAPING THE
PROPELLER —
1/4" X 3-1/2" X 6-1/2"

2-1/4"

HUB —
1-1/2" X 2" X 2"

Forever Grinding

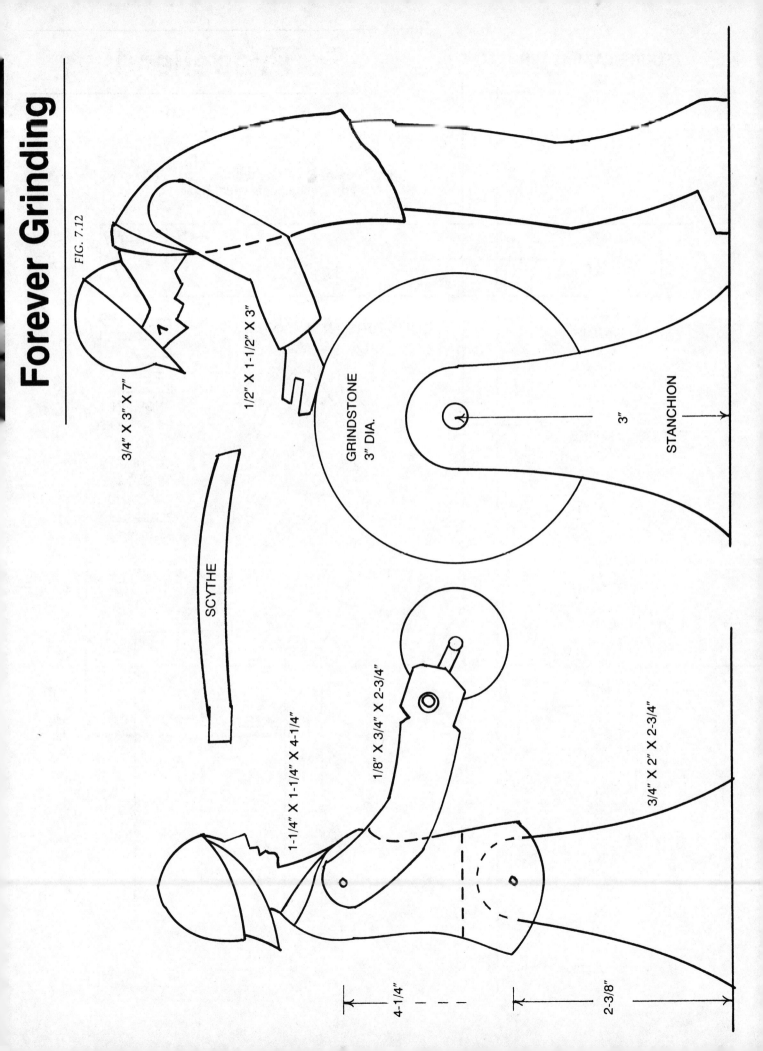

FIG. 7.12

3/4" X 3" X 7"

1/2" X 1-1/2" X 3"

SCYTHE

GRINDSTONE
3" DIA.

STANCHION

3"

1-1/4" X 1-1/4" X 4-1/4"

1/8" X 3/4" X 2-3/4"

3/4" X 2" X 2-3/4"

4-1/4"

2-3/8"

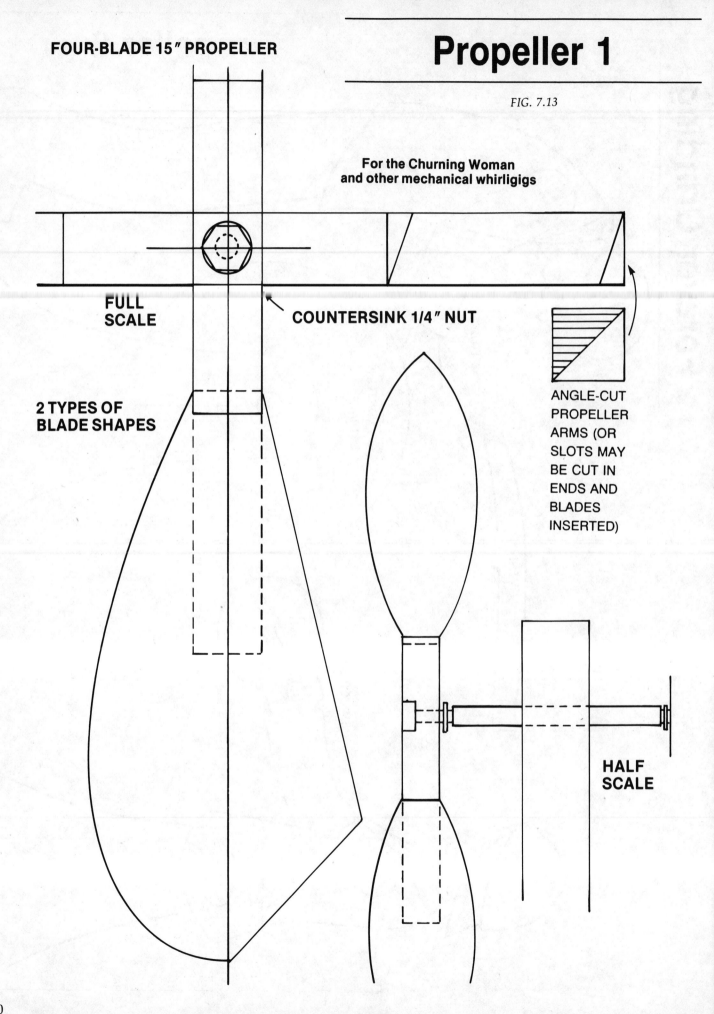

FOUR-BLADE 15" PROPELLER

Propeller 1

FIG. 7.13

**For the Churning Woman
and other mechanical whirligigs**

**FULL
SCALE**

COUNTERSINK 1/4" NUT

**2 TYPES OF
BLADE SHAPES**

**ANGLE-CUT
PROPELLER
ARMS (OR
SLOTS MAY
BE CUT IN
ENDS AND
BLADES
INSERTED)**

**HALF
SCALE**

FOUR-BLADE 12″ PROPELLER

FIG. 7.14

**For the Signaling Trainman
and other mechanical
whirligigs**

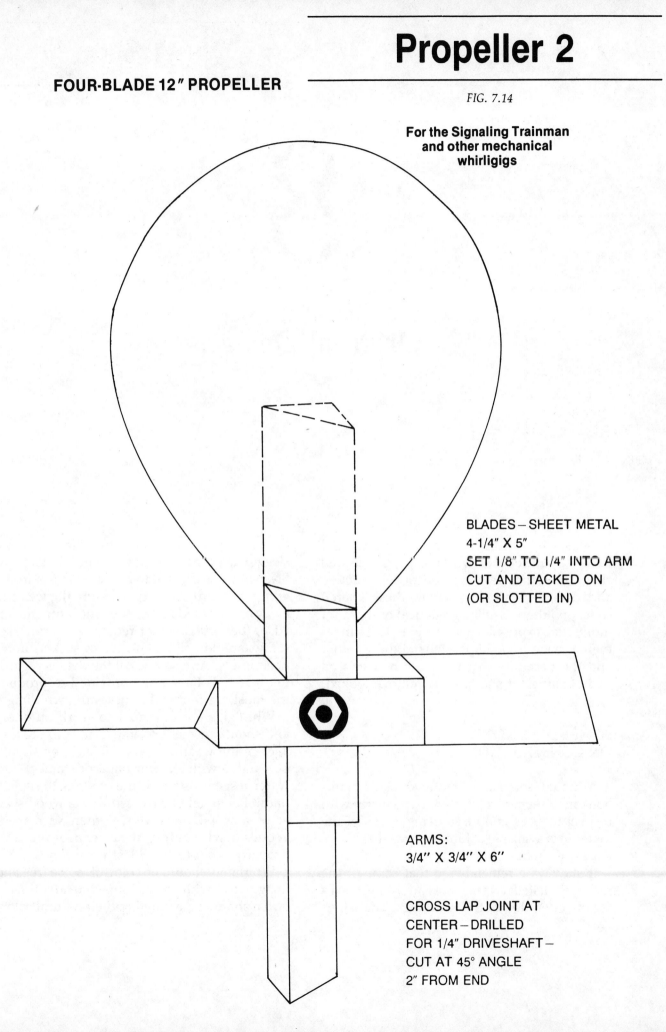

BLADES — SHEET METAL
4-1/4″ X 5″
SET 1/8″ TO 1/4″ INTO ARM
CUT AND TACKED ON
(OR SLOTTED IN)

ARMS:
3/4″ X 3/4″ X 6″

CROSS LAP JOINT AT
CENTER — DRILLED
FOR 1/4″ DRIVESHAFT —
CUT AT 45° ANGLE
2″ FROM END

8

Developing
Original Designs

While some whirligigs may be complex and have a multitude of working parts, they all share the same basic concepts of construction and design. However, within these shared concepts, there is still a great deal of room for individual expression, so long as the fundamental need to be impervious to the weather and the necessity that the parts be balanced and of sufficient strength are not overlooked.

SOME FINAL NOTES ON CONSTRUCTION

Although some of the materials listed in this book may seem complicated, particularly with respect to sizes and measurements, all of the material is available at lumberyards, hardware stores, or hobby shops.

It should be remembered that some of the materials listed are not absolutely necessary for the operation of the whirligigs. The wings

do not need sleeves at the hubs and the sleeves need not be of a specific dimension. Sleeves are suggested to prevent wear, but the wings will turn a long time before the wearing away of the wood makes them non-functional. Also, the hub does not require a specific size screw; an old nail will do. Pivot sockets don't need liners. And so on. All the details regarding materials have been provided to produce the most efficient and long-lasting whirligigs.

Whirligigs are designed to work outdoors and should be made as impervious to the ravages of the weather as possible. They should be painted with exterior paint or stained with water-resistant stain. If the wood is to remain natural, it should be treated with a wood sealer or a wood preservative, then varnished. Wooden whirligigs, weatherproofed and properly cared for, will last for years.

Whirligigs should be colorful, so be free and imaginative with color. Some, like identifiable birds, should be painted in their natural colors according to their natural patterns, but others can be painted in a cheerful variety of attention-getting hues.

REPAIRING WHIRLIGIGS

Repairing whirligigs is not difficult. Made of wood, whirligig parts can be replaced easily. Broken propellers can be rebuilt. A common problem is a loose screw, which can cause a counterclockwise propeller to fall off or a clockwise propeller to tighten and stick. The wing- or propeller-base hole should be filled with wood and glue or with wood filler, and the screw replaced. With arm-waving types, arms can work loose on the ends of the axles. The holes can be filled in with wood filler or with epoxy cement to hold firm when the arms are replaced.

Driveshafts on mechanical whirligigs should be kept lubricated, and a few drops of oil should occasionally be placed in all propeller hubs.

DEVELOPING NEW DESIGNS

Whenever you are traveling and see a whirligig, stop to study it. Measure it and record its dimensions. Pay particular attention to any mechanism new to you and try to understand how it works. If it is unusual, sketch or photograph the whirligig. If it is the work of a local person, talk to that person if you can. Craftspeople are craftspeople the world over, and they like to talk about their work and exchange ideas.

A number of museums, particularly those with collections of folk art, have whirligigs on display. Visit them whenever you can and study the fascinating wind toys. Many of them found in any given display will be the work of one individual and will be one-of-a-kind. You will learn much about how the designer overcame problems you may be dealing with in your own work. One remarkable collection of antique whirligigs is in the Museum of American Folk Art in New York City.

Index

Page numbers in *italic* indicate information in illustrations.

American Goldfinch, 7
Arm-waving whirligigs, 7–8, *7*, *8*
  construction of, 41–63
    basic steps in, 42–43
    modified propeller models, 49–50, *50*, *51*, 52
    rudder assembly models, 46, 47, 48–49, *48–50*
    standard models, 43–46, *44–47*
Arms, waving, as propellers, 14–15

Balance. *See also* Hub and pivot
  of weathervane, 8, *9*, 65
Birds, 6–7
  models of standard, 23–24, *23*, *24*
Body of whirligig, 12
  for winged whirligig, 11–12, 21–22
Bolts, in driveshafts, *19*, 20

Cardinal, 23–24, *23*, *24*
Carving. *See* Cutting and carving
Churning Woman, 10, 17, 20, 78–79, *78*
Colonial Dame, 48, *48*, 49
Construction, 3–5
  final notes on, 92–93
Cutting and carving
  of arm-waving whirligig, 43
  of weathervane whirligig, 65

Danny the Dragon, 23, *23*
Design, 3, 4, 21
  of arm-waving whirligig, 42
  developing original, 92–93
  of weathervane whirligig, 64–65
Doggie, 49, *50*
Drafting, copying, and drawing, 4
Driveshaft for mechanical whirligig, *19*, *20*, 81

Eastern Bluebird, 23, *24*

Fan, 4
Flower Lady, 46, *46*, 47
Flying Puffin, 25, *25*, 26–27
Flying Witch, 9, *66*, 67
Forever Grinding, 80–82, *80–82*

General George Washington, 7, *7*
Gentleman Jim, 45–46, *45*, *46*
Georgine and Her Flying Machine, 67–69, *68*

Halley's Comet, 69–70, *70*
Hub, 14, *14*, 22
  pivot and
    for arm-waving whirligig, 42–43
    in correct relationship, 7–8, *8*

Indian in Canoe, *51, 52*

Mallard Duck, 24
Man Rowing Boat, 4–5, 50, 50–51, 52
Materials for construction, 3
Mechanical whirligigs, 9–10, *10, 11*
    construction of, 77–91
      basic steps, 77–78
      individual models, 78–82
    driveshafts for, *19, 20*
    propellers for 17–18, *18*
Modern Times, 27–28, *27*
Mounting stand, 3, *4*
    for painting, 23, *23*

Nanny the Goat, 25, *27*

Painting of winged whirligigs, 23
Patterns
    for arm-waving whirligig, 42
    for weathervane whirligig, 65
Pegasus, 25, 26–27, *27*
Pinwheel, 2, *2*
Pivot point, 12–13, *13,* 22
    hub and
      for arm-waving whirligig, 42–43
      in correct relationship, 7–8, *8*
    of weathervane, 8, *9,* 65
Platform for mechanical whirligig, 80–81
Propeller(s), 9, *9,* 13–20
    basic style of, 13–14, *14*
    elongated, 27, *27*
    for mechanical whirligigs, 17–18, *18,* 81–82, *82*
    metal, 16, *17*
    modified, 14–15, *15*
      for arm-waving whirligigs, 49–50, *50, 51*
    multibladed, 15–16, *15, 16*
    new designs of, 18, *18,* 20
    principle for design and construction of, 7
    repair of, 93

Repair of whirligigs, 93
Rod shaft, *19,* 20
Rudder, 8
Rudder assembly models, 46, 47–50, *48–49*

Santa, 48, 49, *50*
Sawing. *See* Cutting and carving

Seagull, 7, 24
Ships as weathervanes, 67
Signaling Sailor, 44–45, *44*
Signaling Trainman, 17, 20, 79–80, *79*
Soldier, 46, *48*
Split-wing models, 25, *25*
Stand, *See* Mounting stand
Standing Puffin, 26, *26*

Tail assembly, 8
Tools, 3

Uncle Sam, 43, 44, *44*

Weathervane whirligigs, 8–9, *9*
    construction of, 64–76
      basic steps in, 64–65, *65*
      models for, 65, *66,* 67–70
      summary of material sizes for, 69t., *71–76*
Whirligig
    basic parts of, 12–20, *12*
      body, 12
      pivot, 12–13, *13*
      propellers, 13–20, *14–18*
      wing base, 12, *13*
    construction of, 3–5
    design of, 3
    introduction to, 1–2
    origin of word, 7
    original, 2
    repairing, 93
    types of, 6–10, *6–11. See also* Arm-waving whirligigs;
        Mechanical whirligigs; Winged whirligigs
Willy the Whale, 9, *66,* 67
Windmill, 1, *1,* 15, 70, *70*
Wing base of whirligig, 12, *13,* 22
    construction of, 22
Winged whirligigs, 6–7, *7*
    construction of, 21–40
      basic steps in, 21–23, *22, 23*
      modified wing models, 27–28, *27*
      split-wing models, 25, *25*
      standard bird models, 23–24, *23, 24*
      summary of material sizes for 28t., *29–40*
Wings, construction of, 22–23, *22*
Wood for bodies and frames, 3